The Witch Way

to Manifest

Vix Marie

To Mother Goose,

For showing me The Witch Way

Contents

1. Introduction — 5
2. What is a Witch? — 7
3. The Universal Laws — 12
4. Intention (Step 1) — 30
5. Decluttering (Step 2) — 38
6. Environmental Changes (Step 3) — 49
7. Feel the Vibe and Avoid a Spiral (Steps 4 and 5) — 52
8. Expanders and Role Models (Step 6) — 61
9. Gratitude — 64
10. Manifesting vs Spellwork — 69
11. Grounding and Protection — 71
12. Deities and Goddesses — 75
13. Altars and Your Sacred Space — 80
14. Elements — 83
15. Magickal Correspondences — 88
16. Moon Phases and Rituals — 110
17. Menstruation Magick, Womb Wisdom and Sexual Power — 120

18. Magickal and Psychological Tools (Step 7)　127

19. Spells and Manifestation Boosters　137

20. Self-Love, Receiving and Detachment (Steps 8 & 9)　177

21. Aligned Action (Step 10)　184

22. Dive Deeper - Work with Vix Marie　196

23. Acknowledgements　198

Introduction

Hello, my loves! Welcome to this scrumptious little book that will change your life. Whether you are a baby witch, professional witch, newbie witch or never heard of witches' witch, this book will help you learn how to manifest and work with the universal laws like you never have before.

I spent years in the broom closet. I was afraid to claim my witchy status, but as I explain in the first chapter, this is not nearly as sinister (or OTT) as Hollywood would have us believe.

You can dip in and out of the chapters as you feel called to, and also use it as a reference point in the future when you are in need of a refresh or a spell recap. In the first instance, I would guide you to read the chapters in order, so that you have an understanding of the foundations and their origins before jumping straight into your cauldron. This will also help you appreciate and embody a deeper level of manifestation practice. The tools are great, and also a lot of fun to work with, but we want to be doing the higher-level work on your mindset and energetics to ensure success and longevity.

I also want to take this opportunity to say thank you, but I honestly don't know how to write this in a way that could even begin to express my gratitude to you. Firstly, for being so open to reading a book written by a witch, and for approaching this with an open heart and mind. That is something that has not always been my reality or people's approach to what I have to say. I was quite frankly shitting myself about putting my name on this book, sharing my magick and shouting up about a different way to manifest and work alongside the universe in a conscious and loving way that benefits all beings.

My own journey is ongoing too. As a fellow human, I am continuing to release those ancestral wounds that have taught us to be quiet, a good girl and not say boo to a goose. That being a witch is a bad thing. That women especially should not be seen, heard or in powerful positions. And my own limiting beliefs that I am not good enough to be a coach, a mentor, a speaker and an author. Well, here I am. I am doing it. Living it. Breathing it. And you can do what you desire too.

Secondly, I want to thank you for being curious and committed enough to take conscious, intentional, deliciously aligned action towards your own goals by buying this book to support you on your path. I am so proud of you. I know it is not always easy to face up to the work that is required to really get the lifestyle you wish for, but once you start putting all of these steps in to practice, and learning which tools suit you best, your manifestations will fly to you at record breaking broomstick speed!

I hope that in some way I am able to help you to feel your own power and embrace the natural magick and healing that is available to us all, if we just open our soul to it. This is the witch way.

I always welcome messages and would love to hear from you, so feel free to reach out to me on social media and get in touch with your witchy goings on. I wish you all the juicy manifestations in the world and hope that this book allows you to create a life full of magick, love and joy.

From my heart to yours, thank you.

What is a Witch?

In the words of Devon Cole, a witch is a *'woman in total control of herself'*. And to be fair, that is a pretty good way of describing it. However, men can be witches too! We just typically refer to witches as women due to our stronger connection to nature through menstruation and our intuition being generally heightened (thank you biology). But the craft and this book is absolutely open to everyone.

For me, I never really labelled myself until more recent years. I went to a Church of England school. My parents aren't particularly religious and definitely not Pagan. Although, mum is a trained holistic therapist and Reiki practitioner, dad is a keen gardener, and my nan was a midwife (and practicing witch I discovered not so long ago). So, you could say the woo woo and healing nature is in my blood. I was one of those kids who collected rose petals in the garden and made perfume. I spoke to my imaginary friends. I had 'rock pets' that I kept in a butty box and later buried in the garden. All of which is actually witchcraft. I was also often at the centre of some peculiar goings on and what might be described as 'haunting' activities. None of it particularly phased me, but mum was less than pleased when the bath would run itself and mirrors would be covered in water! I never did like that house...

As I went through puberty and into my early teens, I had a mentor and fellow witch come into my life (RIP Mother Goose). We would 'play' with psychometry and Tarot and practice telepathy. Halloween became my favourite time of year (Samhain) as we would spend weeks preparing her house for the best parties ever, and as I got older, putting the world to rights over a bottle or three of Pinot. I later sought out training opportunities in magick and psychic development. (I spell magick with a 'K' by the way, to differentiate from stage magic and illusion tricks) and worked with some of the best clairvoyants and mediums to help me develop my gifts.

If you are wondering if you are gifted too or could be classed as a witch, let me ask you:

Have you ever made a wish when you blow out candles on a birthday cake? (Fire magick)

Have you ever wished upon a star? (Celestial magick)

Have you ever spoke to the moon or admired her beauty? (Lunar magick)

Have you ever said a prayer? (Manifestation magick)

Have you ever slept with a tooth under your pillow for the tooth fairy to visit? (Pillow magick)

You get the idea, my little witchy friend! There is nothing majorly complex about being a magickal being, it is all about coming back to nature, reconnected to mother earth and listening to our own intuition as a guide.

Our ancestors were traditionally more open to their nature practices and working with the planet as they had few other resources to utilise. Up until the church and state at the time decided plant medicine wasn't going to make them any money (this was before the pharmaceutical industry existed) and women were getting 'too powerful', as they were reluctant to marry and become the property of the men in town. And so, they started the witch hunts! This story could be a whole other book but I often chat about this (OK, rant) on my socials!

Regardless of our ancestors being suppressed (and frequently persecuted), we still have this DNA passed down in our lineage, no matter your heritage. We intuitively know what will help in any given situation. We always, always feel better after spending time in nature. Why? Because it reminds your soul that you are connected and supported by the magick of the universe.

So other than being a little kooky and highly gifted, what does it mean to be a witch?

In the dictionary, we are deemed to have dark powers and can often be seen in a pointed hat and riding a broomstick. In reality, we do have powers; every being on this planet does. And we can use those powers, in conjunction with the elements and nature, to manipulate and create what we desire (aka manifestation). The broomstick connection comes from a pagan fertility ritual to help crops grow and is now a symbol of luck. The hat actually descends from the Judenhat and a fashion statement from the Quakers which Hollywood later adopted as a witchy representation, along with the green skin, crooked nose and warts. Not too far removed from what our sisters would have looked like after the torture they endured before being trialled and killed for witchcraft! Nice.

As these women were often the midwives, medicine women and the caring, nurturing girl next door, it is safe to say we are good people. We heal, help and connect with mama earth to make the world a better place. White and black magick doesn't exist (this actually stems from some rather racist connotations). Magick is magick. We work alongside the elements of spirit, earth, air, fire and water, which are depicted in the famous protective pentagram. I would be lying if I said all magick is "good". There are some practitioners who will explore their dark side and their shadow through their magick and practices. There is no judgement with the craft. We all have a shadow, we all get pissed off, and if you hurt me or my loved ones I make no promises as to how my human self would react. We have to be comprised of light and dark, yin and yang, otherwise we are not complete or true to who we are.

Some witches follow a pagan path or wiccan beliefs and enjoy traditional magick and rituals. Others forge their own path to improve their life and the lives of those around them. I personally mix both, as the eclectic witch that I am. There are no strict rules when it comes to being a witch, a pagan or a wiccan. It is not a religion. It is simply nature-based beliefs. (Hello law of attraction!) The only suggested, and very much encouraged, guidance is the rule of three… everything we put out into the world, comes back to us threefold. Therefore, it is my duty as your witchy mentor to remind you to harm none. Your magick must not bring about harm or take away freewill from another. This is not to say you can't banish someone for your own protection (pop them in the freezer!) or remind someone that their actions also have consequences. Just remember, things will come back to you so play smart. And as always, be careful what you wish for…

Being a modern-day witch is not just about casting spells and brewing potions. It's about embracing the power of nature, the cycles of the moon, and the energy within ourselves. It's about finding balance and connecting with the world around us. It's about taking control of our own lives and manifesting our desires.

But most importantly, being a witch is about self-discovery and personal empowerment. It's about embracing our unique gifts and talents and using them to create positive change in the world.

So, if you're feeling called to explore your inner witch, know that it's about delving deep within yourself, connecting with the natural world, and using your intuition to guide you on your path. It's about being true to yourself and living a life that is authentic and fulfilling.

Ready to embrace your inner wisdom? Let the magick begin!

The Universal Laws

Ok, so this is the nerdy kind of bit. Depending on where you do your research, there are many, many universal laws. Gravity is one you have probably heard of! The term "universal laws" can refer to several different concepts in different fields. Some of the most commonly referred to universal laws include:

1. The Laws of Physics - including Newton's laws of motion, the law of universal gravitation, and the laws of thermodynamics.
2. The Laws of Mathematics - including mathematical operations such as addition, subtraction, multiplication, and division.
3. The Laws of Nature - including laws related to biology, chemistry, and ecology.
4. Universal Spiritual Laws - including laws such as the Law of Attraction, the Law of Karma, and the Law of One.

For the purpose of our spiritual education, I am going to introduce you to the 13 that are most common in the world of magick – the spiritual laws. Derived from Hermetic philosophy, you could think of them as the divine guidelines that helps us understand how the universe and everyone in it interacts in a physical and mystical way. Again, you can remove any religious element to this as you wish. You can also replace the term 'universe' with God, or any other deity or cosmic being you desire. By having an understanding of these laws, you can see how the most famous one, the law of attraction, should not be the sole focus. We want to have an awareness of all of them just to build up our knowledge base.

1. Law of Divine Oneness

This is the reminder that we are all connected. Remember the threefold guidance? Harm none as otherwise you will feel it too…

The Law of Divine Oneness, also known as the Law of One, is a spiritual belief that states that all things in the universe are interconnected and that everything is ultimately one and the same. According to this law, there is no separation between the individual and the universe, and the universe is seen as a single, unified whole. Which is why the universe will always have your back and want the best for you.

Every individual is a unique expression of the universe, and every experience is a reflection of the greater whole. All living beings, including humans, animals and plants, are part of this interconnected whole and we all are connected to each other and to the universe. You may have heard that trees are all interconnected and that their roots all link together underground so they can actually communicate to one another. This law is the same concept.

It is often associated with a belief in the interconnectedness of all things and a recognition of the interdependence of all life. This is a key principle for understanding the nature of reality and our place within it. I also find it really helpful when I need a bit of perspective or a reminder that when someone is being a pillock, we are all one. It can be beneficial in helping to accept one another in both our good and bad frames of mind.

How good does it feel when you help someone out or make someone else smile? Great! Because we are all connected. How does it feel when you hurt someone or do something sneaky? Grim! Because we are all connected. Try to recognise this and be more compassionate and understanding towards others.

This is where we are able to help and support others through our magick and manifesting too. We are able to heal the collective and make the world a better place simply because we are all one. Remember this whenever you feel helpless and like you can't make a difference in the world. You can.

How does this law make you feel initially? Do you like the thought of us all being connected or do you prefer a degree of separation? Why?

How could this law support you in your manifesting efforts and your relationships with others?

2. Law of Vibration

We are all made of energy. Every little atom and particle of your being is vibrating at a certain frequency. Everything in the universe vibrates at a particular frequency, including thoughts, emotions, and physical matter.

According to this law, everything vibrates at a unique frequency. These frequencies determine the manifestation of matter in the physical world. By raising our vibration, we can attract more positive experiences and abundance into our lives.

When we are happy, we vibrate quicker (and things flow to us faster as a result). When we are sad, we vibrate slower (and results can take longer to come into fruition). We talk about our vibe later in this book as we want to shift our vibration to the same level as our desires to that they can reach us.

This is why when something happens in the morning that lowers our mood (stepping on a plug, running out of toothpaste etc), we typically find something else will happen that is equally as unpleasant (you spill your coffee, get stuck in traffic) because your vibration has been lowered to the frequency of unpleasant things. The trick is to let the sucky, low vibration stuff go, as quick as is feasible for you. See how long you can stay on a higher vibe for the morning. If you make it to 8am one day, try for 8.30am the next day, 9am the next day, and so on. Eventually you will be a whizz at keeping that vibe high! This is why yoga, meditation, sound baths and chakra healing are so popular- they lift that vibrational energy fast! More on this in chapter 7.

3. Law of Action

Yep, you do actually have to take action. As nice as it would be to just sit back and wait for our manifestations to be delivered to our doorstep, we have to show the universe we mean business. In order to achieve a desired outcome, we must take action towards it, as well as not sabotaging our intentions by taking steps away from it.

This law holds that simply thinking about a goal or desire is not enough (soz). According to the Law of Action, thoughts and ideas are potential energy. It is only through taking action that this potential energy can be transformed into tangible results. This means that it is necessary to take action in order to turn desires into realities.

The Law of Action is often associated with the idea that success requires both planning and action. (Which also works with the Law of Gender as this is feminine and masculine combined).
It is believed that a person can have the best intentions and plans, but unless they take action towards their goals, they will not be successful, and life would also be pretty boring.

So, we are encouraged to take the actions that our human form allows us to do. Want to release some weight? Start moving. Want to attract a new job? Start applying. Want to find a partner? Go on a date. I call this aligned action. Human nature can often mean our ego gets us to take unaligned action in a bid to keep us safe and comfortable right where we are. We can also self-sabotage to stay in this 'safe place'. I love diving into my client's sabotage mode (there are six FYI) but a great tip to help you is this- with every action you take, ask yourself, *"Is this aligned with what I want to achieve and manifest?"* More on this later too.

What actions are you currently taking towards your goals?

Are you taking steps that support your manifestations or that are moving you further away?

Have you procrastinated at any point? Why do you think this is?

4. Law of Correspondence

Bitter pill to swallow here! Anything that we dislike in someone else, is a reflection of our inner psyche. Anything we love in someone else, is a reflection of our own traits. Think of it like a mirror. Your reality is a reflection, or physical manifestation, of your inner world. If there is chaos around you, there is chaos within you. *"As above, so below"*; *"As it is inside, so it will be outside"*. In other words, we must change our inner world to change the outer world. As the wonderful healer, Louise Hay said, *"The thoughts we think and the words we speak create our experiences."* Needless to say, affirmations and mantras are powerful AF.

This law states that there is a correspondence between the inner and outer worlds. This means that what we experience in our inner world (our thoughts, emotions, and beliefs) is reflected in our outer world (our physical reality).

The Law of Correspondence is often associated with the idea that we create our own reality through our thoughts, beliefs, and emotions. So, by shifting our inner state (and energy), we can create positive changes in our outer world.

This law is the key for you to be aware of in order to manifest things that you actually want and to do it from the inside out! Clients often have a bit of a panic with this one as well as the law of vibration. They worry that when they are not feeling so good about themselves, they are going to attract all of the things that they don't want. But remember, manifestations can take time. Life is happening for you, not to you. We are all one, so the universe wants good things for you! Manifestations will naturally take a longer time when we are low vibe because our energy is slower. I have tested this even in my high vibe states when trying to manifest Chris Hemsworth to pop around for tea and biscuits. He has not (yet) instantly appeared in my kitchen! Use these reflections, along with your own feelings (and vibe) as signposts as to what you need to change. You can also work with natural correspondences, as is the witch way, to enhance your work, which I will explain later.

What do you dislike about your reality right now?

Where do you think this has stemmed from?

Is there anything about the people around you that you don't particularly like?

Do you recognise any of these traits within yourself?

5. Law of Attraction

Ahh, the biggie that we have all probably heard of, thanks to books like *The Secret* and the movie of the same name (both of which I recommend, by the way but also can miss out some integral information which I hope to bring you in this book).

This law is usually what we focus on when it comes to manifesting. That is where you can miss out on a few tricks. The Law of Attraction is simply this- like attracts like. What we give out, is what we get back (x3). It is getting all your ducks in a row and aligning your thoughts and actions.

This law holds that we are magnets - attracting into our lives experiences, people, and circumstances that match our thoughts and emotions. It is often applied to personal development and goal setting, with the belief that by focusing on a desired outcome we can attract it into our lives.

People often get frustrated that the Law of Attraction isn't working. It is… whether you are consciously working with it or not. The same with all of these laws. They are happening all of the time. Have you ever floated off into space? No? The law of gravity is always working (phew!) We just choose whether or not to have some input. The biggest challenge I see with the Law of Attraction, other than not considering the other laws, is that people wait before they act. They expect to have the desire before being that person. We have to flip that around. Be the person who we are manifesting. Act like that person and the universe will deliver.

Let me explain this in a little more detail. Trying to change other people or the world around you is a long hard slog that no witch has time for. The key is the change yourself.

Believing that your desires are even possible for you to have. Accept your current situation, no matter how much you may dislike it. Look for the good. Look for the lessons. Focus on where you are heading. Your power lies in changing **you** (with the help of many, many witchy boosters that you will learn soon). Be the person you want to become **now** and your external circumstances will soon reflect this too.

What are you attracting at this present moment?

What thoughts are leading to these manifestations?

How does this make you feel?

Who would you rather be?

How could you already be like them?

What would that feel like instead?

6. Law of Cause and Effect

The direct correlation between your actions and intentions and what events occur thereafter. That threefold ripple effect is real. This law illustrates how everything that happens to us always has a reason behind it. Remember the movie, The Butterfly Effect? This is the spiritual law behind it.

According to this law, our actions and thoughts are seeds that we plant. The results we experience in life are the fruit of these seeds. All of our actions, both positive and negative, have consequences and we are responsible for these consequences. We create our own reality through our actions, and our experiences are a result of the choices we have made in the past. (In this life or ones prior!)

Coming back to that Law of Divine Oneness- our actions can also impact on others, whether good or bad. Let's say you ate a family size KFC bucket and a Pizza Hut buffet, followed by 3 packets of cookies and half a tub of ice cream (cause). You then hopped on the scales the morning after to find your weight had increased (effect). From this, you then have a go at your partner for 'allowing you' to eat so much, sulk with them for the rest of the day and make them feel bad in the process (ripple). Change the cause, i.e., your actions, and you will change the effect, i.e., the result.

What effects do you see around you?

Can you identify the cause?

What is the ripple that happens as a result?

7. Law of Compensation

You get as good as you give; similar to other laws we have mentioned. The universe wants to reward you for what you do. I like to think of this like being the star employee for the universe.

What would the universe have you do today to make the world a better place?

Your life will then be rewarded positively. This gives us purpose and encouragement to do good.

The universe provides us with what we need in proportion to what we give. According to this law, we receive a reward or compensation for every action we take, good or bad. By giving to others, whether it be time, resources, or positive energy, we will receive a corresponding reward. This reward may come in many forms, such as financial compensation, personal growth, or increased happiness.

This can sometimes be a bit of a hurdle, and to be honest, is the law I find most challenging- especially when bad things happen to good people. Why were our ancestors and sisters killed for helping and healing others in their village? Why do our loved ones get sick? Why does war and terrorism exist that hurts innocent people?

If I am honest, I don't have the full answer, other than the other universal laws would always be in play. Should there be fear within us, that fear will manifest externally. Should there be repressed feelings, anger or resentment within us (aka a witch wound!) then these often manifest as sickness in a way of trying to release these feelings.

This is another reason that Reiki and chakra healing are so powerful as they remove any physical blocks in our energy centres before they physically manifest. If you have ever had a nervous tummy and active bowel as a result, your solar plexus (energy centre) was trying to release the self-doubt. If you have ever had lower back or knee pain, your root chakra is trying to release fear of instability. Period pains and cramps are a sacral release of all trauma held in the womb. This is another book entirely (that will be manifested soon...), but you see where I am coming from.

One thing I love about this law, is the association with abundance and the belief that there is enough for everyone. Through focusing on abundance and giving to others, we can attract more abundance into our own lives too.

How would you like to give more to others?

In what ways would you love to be compensated?

How can you become the star employee of the week for the universe?

8. Law of Perpetual Transmutation of Energy

What a mouthful! In simple terms, this means our energy is able to shift from high to low and vice versa. For example, when you are feeling a little down and a friend pops over to cheer you up, they transmutate your energy to a higher frequency. Or on the flip side, when you are feeling really good but spend a day in endless meetings with people unhappy in their job, you leave the office feeling depleted and much lower energy than when you arrived at work.

Energy cannot be created or destroyed, only transformed. According to this law, all energy is in constant motion and constantly changing form. This law is often applied to personal growth and development, with the belief that by transforming negative energy into positive energy, we can create positive change in our lives.

To work with this positively, seek out those higher energy people and environments as often as you can. '*Your vibe attracts your tribe.*' Who are you choosing to hang out with? They should lift your spirit, not drain it. The same for your home environment. It should be rejuvenating not exhausting to be in your home. We will talk about this more later.

What energy around you would you like to transform?

How could you alter the energetic state within you?

In what ways do you feel the energy around you could be changed?

9. Law of Relativity

We are being tested by the universe. Yay!

What this means is, the universe is testing our perspective. It is part of our human journey to label things as 'good' or 'bad' when in actual fact, it is neutral, until we give it meaning. More often than not, our meaning or labelling of a situation comes from comparing to others rather than connecting to our own voice and interpretation.

For example, if we're feeling ungrateful for our work situation, it could be because we're comparing our job role with someone else's. Instead, we could appreciate what we have for the learning and development it provides us. Comparisonitus can be a real drag and has a lot to answer for when it comes to manifestation. Not only does it lower your energy and vibration, it is also demotivating, a knock to your self esteem and it suppresses the Law of Relativity.

Change your perspective, you can change your life. Remember it is our thoughts that determine how we feel. It is how we feel (our emotions) that influence how we act and behave. So, ultimately your thoughts are the cause of your reality. (Law of Attraction proven by neuroscience!)

Where do you tend to compare yourself to others?

What impact does this have on you? And how you feel or act?

Is this beneficial? How can it bring you a better perspective?

10. Law of Rhythm

Everything has a rhythm. A pattern or a cycle. The seasons. Menstruation. We are cyclical beings and cycles are a natural component of the universe. According to this law, everything experiences highs and lows, ebbs and flows, and has its own unique rhythm.

This principle applies to all aspects of life, including personal growth, relationships and finances. By understanding and working with the rhythms of life, we can achieve greater balance, harmony, and success. Everything moves in a natural and predictable rhythm. By recognising and aligning with these rhythms, we can achieve greater flow and harmony in our lives.

When we expect to be able to maintain the same state, or be consistently 'on', all of the time, we are going against this law. For women especially, we are guided to listen to our natural rhythm and hormonal cycle. It is not natural for us to be 'on' and hustle all of the time. It will only lead to exhaustion and disappointment. Allow yourself to flow. Connecting to the cycles of the seasons, the moon and your own hormones will show you how and when to best manifest your desires. Check out chapters 16 and 17 for more support on this.

Are you currently aware of your natural rhythms?

Do you acknowledge or ignore your own energy cycle?

In what ways could you alter your daily or weekly schedule to accommodate your own ebb and flow?

How do you feel when you are in flow?

Is this better or worse than when you are still? Why?

11. Law of Polarity

There are two sides to everything. A coin. A magnet. A situation. A person. One cannot exist without the other. For example, love and hate, joy and sadness, and good and evil are opposite poles of the same concept.

Every concept, experience, and object has a counterpart on the opposite end of the spectrum. This applies to all aspects of life, including emotions, thoughts, and actions. By understanding the Law of Polarity, we can create greater balance and harmony in our lives.

This law shows us that in order to attract the 'positive' pole, we must accept the existence and purpose of the 'negative' pole. In darkness we can find light. Those hard times show us how great the better times are. We would struggle to understand what success is without experiencing failure. We would not truly know or value love without there being hate. We have a choice which side of the coin we focus on and how we navigate the 'negative' sides of life. If you can see adversity and pain as lessons and part of your human journey, you will grow and develop so much more, as well as appreciating those more 'positive' moments.

Which end of the 'pole' are you currently experiencing in your life right now? Think about in your career, relationships, health, finances etc.

How can you use this as guidance, inspiration or a developmental opportunity?

12. Law of Gender

There is masculine and feminine energy that exists in us all. Our yin and yang. In the western world, we are conditioned to live very much in our masculine, 'doing' energy. This supresses our feminine flow and the ability to just 'be'.

Both are connected and equally important. We cannot live without them both. Our feminine energy allows us to look inwards, to create and to hear our intuition. The masculine allows us to take action, to achieve and to showcase ourselves to the world. It is the feminine that is the energy of manifestation as we are in receiving mode. It is the masculine that allows us to hold and maintain what we receive.

If you find you are constantly on the go, that your ego is running the show or that you are reaching the point of exhaustion, you are too far in your masculine. If you are experiencing a lot of emotions, feeling overwhelmed and unable to motivate yourself to take action, you are too far in the feminine. Balance the two with daily practices (for example, lists, plans and workouts for the masculine. Journaling, bathing and gardening for the feminine) and also coming back to your own rhythm and cycle. This harmonious way of living is exactly the balance we hope to achieve through living 'The Witch Way'.

What would you say is your dominant energy?

How could you benefit from more of a balance?

What activities might you like to try to help you?

13. Law of Detachment

The Law of Detachment is a concept in spirituality and personal development, which states that in order to achieve happiness and inner peace, we must let go of attachment to material possessions, outcomes and emotions. It is believed that attachment causes suffering and that, by detaching from these things, an individual can achieve a state of inner freedom and contentment.

This concept is often associated with spiritual practices and belief systems such as Buddhism, Hinduism, and Taoism. It is also a common principle in many self-help and personal growth programs. The idea is that by letting go of attachment, one can become more present and focused on the present moment, which will help to live life with a greater sense of peace and purpose.

From a manifestation perspective, I always explain this law with a restaurant analogy. Once we have selected what we would like from the menu, made any special requests and placed our order, we sit back and continue to enjoy the experience. We wouldn't (I hope) keep going into the kitchen to ask the chef how long they are going to be with the order. We live in the moment and trust that the chef will do their job, and the waiter will deliver our order at the perfect, divine time.

Sometimes clients struggle with this one a little bit as they misinterpret detachment for inaction. You can still get your cutlery and napkins ready for when your order arrives, and you don't walk out of the restaurant if your meal isn't delivered within 30 seconds. Have trust in the universe and do your part but don't dwell. Trust like a cat who knows he is always getting his next meal, treats and pets!

Write down any other thoughts that have come up for you when learning about the Universal Laws. How might you like to work with these more consciously moving forwards?

Intention

The most powerful part of a witch's toolkit is our intention, and this is step one in my manifestation process. It is really important that you get crystal clear on your intention and what it is that you want to manifest. The universe will figure out the logistics of how to deliver it to you, but your order needs to be clear so that there is no confusion or miscommunication. As a collective I think it is pretty safe to say we have been trying to manifest a bit of a break from work and being able to hibernate at home or have a duvet day or two. What we didn't expect was for that to present itself as a global pandemic that sent us in to lockdown. Our manifestation worked but not really how we meant…be careful what you wish for!

This is the first step in your manifestation process. Setting an intention is a way of focusing your thoughts and energy towards a specific goal or outcome.

1. Identify what you want: Determine what it is you want to manifest or achieve. Make sure it is specific, measurable (so you will know when you have it), and meaningful to you, not for someone else. It can benefit others but remember- this is *your* intention.

2. Get clear on why it is important to you. Understanding the deeper motivations and values behind your intention can help increase your commitment to it, especially if it doesn't come into fruition as quickly as you'd like it to.

3. What is the pain or pleasure that you are currently experiencing?

As humans, we are always naturally guided away from anything that causes pain and towards anything that will bring pleasure (sexual or otherwise). *What pain does your intention move you away from? What pleasure does it move you towards?*

If you aren't too sure what you want, try these steps:

1. **Identify your values.** Understanding what is most important to you can help guide your decisions and goals. List your top 10 values if you can and then narrow it down to the top 3. If you find this challenging, think about what was most important to you as a child. Maybe love, comfort, or adventure? Has anything changed now you are all grown up? (An example to note: if freedom is your top value but you are thinking you might want to manifest a new job with more responsibilities and an increase in working hours, this might not be aligned with your core desires and will probably not come into fruition as you will subconsciously sabotage it, or you may land the job and not stick with it due to lack of fulfilment. On the other hand, if you decide to manifest a business where you can work and travel at your own pace, you will likely find this flows into your life much easier as it aligns perfectly with your freedom value. Check those values match up to what you want to manifest.)

2. **Reflect on your current life**. Consider what is working well and what areas you would like to improve. This might not be monumental, but it could be an upgrade from economy to premium class. Look at your health and wellbeing; your career or business; your family and home life; your education and development; your finances; love or dating life; friends and social activities as a starting point. You might decide your health is in the most need of an upgrade so look to manifest working with a personal trainer, making environmental changes and incremental upgrades like a new pair of trainers or gym hoody.

3. **Set specific goals.** Make sure your goals are measurable and allow yourself to dream big. People often say, *"Be realistic"* but what is 'realistic' varies from one person to the next. As a coach, I am wary of this realistic goal setting as actually being a mode of self-sabotage, so I say, *"Dream big, moonshine!"* You can do the action planning with the step by step of how you are going to do your part later. Right now, dream it and believe it.

4. Try the following journal prompts or create your own. Allow yourself to hear your inner voice and spend time in quiet contemplation. Ask yourself:

What do I really want?

Why is this important to me?

What would I like to achieve?

What would make the 8-year-old version of me happy?

What would make 80-year-old me proud and content?

What if I don't achieve it?

Is it that important?

If I could be, do or have anything, what would I choose?

What would the universe have me do today/ this week/ this year?

You are then ready to set your intention. Take a brand-new page in your journal or on a piece of paper and write at the top, almost like the title of a book, what your intention is.

Some examples for you:

My new, secure, well-paid job at X company.

My fit and healthy body.

My exciting adventure trip to X.

As you think about your intention, it is also good practice to really consider why you want it… like the real deep reason why. This will help you generate ideas when it comes to thinking of aligned actions to take and also keeping you motivated. I would always advise, especially in the early stages of your manifesting, to focus on intentions that are just for you. This avoids overcomplicating things and also ensures there is no interference with free will. I have often been asked about manifesting to get an ex-partner back. While this is completely possible, it does interfere with that person's own intention and can also block what the universe had in mind for you both. What is better practice, is to focus on the intention of a committed, loving relationship and then let the universe work on the logistics.

I would also flip this to the other side and ask yourself why you don't want it. This will highlight your fears and potential subconscious blocks to work through. These are the areas that self-development, support from coaches and deep subconscious healing can help you eliminate. This also checks your belief in the possibility of the intention coming into fruition. As we now know, if you don't believe in it or truly want it, the universal laws won't be aligned with it for you.

Best to establish this in the first instance before we invest more time and energy into something you don't really want or don't think can happen. If we want to have 6-pack abs but don't think it is feasible for us, our visits to the gym will feel pointless and inevitably we will give up. Get behind your intention.

You will continue to use your intention in all of your practices and spell work. You have already experienced this when you wished on your birthday cake candles. You intended for that wish to come true. Kitchen witches incorporate intention into everything they cook. For me, stirring my cuppa every morning (clockwise to call in, anticlockwise to remove) with the intention of having a great day or removing self-doubt is as easy as magick can be. You can so this when you clean too – wipe your countertops/ sweep your floors clockwise/ to the right to call in, anticlockwise/ to the left to remove.

List some of your current intentions below:

Decluttering

You will love or hate this one, but it is integral to your manifestation success. Step two- we must declutter. Not just physically, but mentally and emotionally as well. I know! I make no apologies for this; we just have to crack on.

Let's start with the easiest part – the physical declutter.

How do you feel when you are surrounded by mess? A bit chaotic? Overwhelmed? It messes with our vibe, not to mention our zen. Parents, I feel you. But we can do our best with this one. Not only is our physical environment a reflection of our inner world, but it also has significant impact on our emotional health and wellbeing too. Delegate what you can if time is precious. At the time of writing this, my lovely cleaner is here with her niece (aka the Dust Queen!) If money doesn't allow, reassess your priorities. I will gladly substitute a monthly takeaway in order to have my house kept clean (and support another woman in business).

Physically decluttering also creates space. One of the ways the law of attraction works is through nature abhorring a vacuum. What this means in English, is that space can't be empty. Remember, those vibrating particles and atoms that the universe is made up of? They have to fill every space as they flow. Have you ever emptied that one drawer in the house that is full of *all* the things, only to find a few days later it is full again? This is the cycle, and this is how you can help your manifestations flow by creating space. Even if it is temporary.

Some physical decluttering can be literal. Say you are manifesting a new car, but your garage is overflowing with junk. Where will your new shiny car live? Or if you are longing for a baby but the spare room is full to the brim. Baby won't be sleeping in your bottom drawer, (it is probably full again by now anyway) so clear out the space. Attracting money? Open a new special bank account for all those extra pennies.

This can also help in a less literal sense as it clears our energetic space too. How nice does it feel to have a tidy wardrobe that isn't jam packed? Or a desk that doesn't have paperwork piled high? It shifts your vibration and allows space for unrelated manifestations to flow in.

Marie Kondo was onto something. Anything that doesn't bring you joy, doesn't belong in your energetic space. Be honest with yourself. Holding onto stagnant energy will block your intentions. What would you rather have?

Remember, we all have different perspectives on what clutter is. Declutter in line with your own standards and expectations. You can only do your best. You still have to live your life and have contents in your home for you and your family. Trust your judgement on what is in the way and what is part of you that belongs there. Witches' houses are as varied as your neighbours. We may live in small spaces with minimal items, or we might live in a mansion filled with books, crystals and nick-nacks. The amount of 'stuff' varies, but it should all make us feel good and be more aligned with the lifestyle we are manifesting.

The second part – emotional/ mental decluttering, can be a little bit trickier.

Those subconscious blocks we looked for earlier are the things we want to declutter. Any baggage from past relationships or experiences. Any ancestral trauma. Any limiting stories and thoughts that have arisen from our conditioning and past situations. We want to clear them out. Our subconscious, or unconscious mind is actually millions of times more powerful than our conscious mind. It is said to be in control of 95% of our lives! And yet, here we are focusing so much energy and attention consciously and wondering why we find it such hard work. Muggle error.

The subconscious mind is a part of the mind that operates below the level of our conscious awareness and is responsible for automatic processes such as breathing, our heartbeat, digestion and the 'fight or flight' response that you may have heard of before.

The challenge that often presents itself is down to our Central Nervous System (CNS) and this fight or flight response. The CNS is responsible for regulating and coordinating all of the body's functions, including both our conscious and subconscious actions. When we are faced with a perceived threat, our subconscious triggers the fight or flight response, which prepares our body to respond to the danger by either fighting or fleeing (or freezing). In the animal kingdom this is essential for survival, but for the vast majority of us, it can be a bit of an interference in every day life where there are minimal threats or dangers to run away from or pop on our boxing gloves for.

As a result this response can actually have a significant impact on our ability to manifest because it can create feelings of fear and anxiety so that we actually see our desires and intentions as a threat to escape from!

One of the first things I do with my clients is help them to identify and recognise when their fight or flight response is being triggered and take steps to calm the CNS so their manifestations can flow.

When we don't calm our CNS and stay in the fight or flight response, our body can remain in a heightened state of stress, which can of course lead to physical and mental health problems. Sometimes this response can also be left 'switched on' if we have had significant threats or traumas in our childhood, particularly up to the age of 7.

For example, say your parents always used to argue about money. They then end up getting a divorce and you have to move out of the family home that you love, and move in to a small apartment. You see both parents struggle financially. Your mum is working multiple jobs and your food, treats and clothing are rationed. Your mind sees money as a danger because it believes it was the cause of the divorce, and the cause for your mum having to work so hard. It was the reason behind having to leave your beloved home and the cause of your poverty. Should you try to manifest money in your adult life without having 'switched off' the fight or flight response, your mind will still see money as a danger and a threat so will do everything in its power (95% worth) to stop you from having this 'dangerous money'. In extreme cases, it may cause us to give up on our desires altogether or to develop a negative attitude towards them.

There are many ways you can connect to your unconscious and also your CNS. You do it every night when you dream. You are doing it right this second as you are breathing. You're not consciously focusing on every inhale and exhale, or every beat of your heart, but your mind does it for you. This is the real magickal spot.

You can connect to this more through practices such as meditation, journaling, affirmations, breathwork etc. This forms a bridge between living in the 3D as a muggle who is fearful, anxious, in lack mindset or scarcity, to connecting to the 4D world of more possibility and something greater that is destined for you. When I work with my clients we progress further into the 5th dimension and the quantum field where we are fully connected to your intuition, your highest self and can literally collapse time to manifest at record speed! For now, let's start building that bridge to the 4th dimension…

I would guide you to sit in a quiet space outside and connect to your body. *Where do you feel tension? Where do you feel you are holding these stories or trauma? If you have any physical ailments, where have these come from? What are your emotions and feelings trying to tell you? Do you believe you are still in a fight or flight response to something from your childhood?*

Some common connections between emotions and beliefs, as identified by one of my favourite teachers, Tony Robbins, are below, but please trust your own thoughts and intuition above and beyond this. You will know your own inner voice as it will be quiet and knowing. Your ego and fears on the other hand will be loud and more boisterous!

Anger – boundaries being crossed. Someone, maybe even you, overstepped the line.

Fear – feeling unprepared for what may or may not happen in the future.

Frustration – take aligned action to get results.

Disappointment – check your goal and expectations are appropriate.

Guilt – not committed as much as you intended.

Boredom – clarify intentions and actions to give you a pick me up.

Unworthy – boost confidence and self-love.

Depression/ Sadness – revaluate what is important, take time to rest.

Lonely – seek connection.

Do any of these resonate with you? What are they signalling for you to change?

Some of my favourite journaling prompts you might like to try to help you declutter:

What would the universe like for me?

What could I do today to feel good/ improve my life?

What is stopping me from achieving my goals? Why?

Who could help or support me on my journey?

Where can I find the ideas and inspiration I need?

When is the best time to start this endeavour?

How can I heal what is in the way?

How can I release what I no longer need?

What stories and thoughts do I believe about X?

What does this cause to happen in my life?

How can I disprove this?

What would I rather believe?

What evidence is there to support this is true?

It is also really lovely to use affirmations, declarations or mantras to solidify your intention and help you reframe those thoughts. Affirmations can sometimes feel too far away from your current situation. I could tell myself ten times a day that I am a billionaire, but if I am working a minimum wage job it may not feel possible yet. Declaring that I am working towards an abundant and prosperous life, however, feels real and true.

The way this works is by helping you to speak directly to your subconscious, especially when you look at your reflection in the mirror at the same time. Vocalising them also creates a new vibration and lifts your energy. This is why many spells include mantras or incantations to shift the energy. Repeating them at least three times increases the potency.

Other ways you can work on decluttering these mental and emotional blocks is through therapy- be it through touch, such as massage and reflexology; talking with a trained professional; or energetic through Reiki and chakra work. Hypnosis and counselling are also popular methods for getting into the subconscious and releasing these road bumps. My favourite is womb healing and witch wound clearing, which is what I do on my retreats. This is by far the most powerful healing I have ever been on the receiving end of (closely followed by Reiki which lifted me out of depression) so for me, this is my go-to and number one recommendation.

You may also like to work with a trusted coach or mentor to help you with the reframing and release of these challenges. I love nothing more than seeing my clients move past what has been holding them back for years and making their futures better and brighter. But remember, without those blocks and the 'darkness,' they would not be able to perceive or fully appreciate the light. We experience things for a reason. What will you learn from your experiences? Will you create a new story? Remember, your intention is your number one power!

This journey is an ongoing one. As we are living a human experience, we will go through those cycles again. We are meant to have highs and lows. We are designed to ebb and flow. Just like the moon. Just like the tides of the ocean. Just like the seasons.

Please do not worry if old stories pop back up when you thought you had released them and let go. You are human, that is normal. If things pop back up it is so you can learn something new and grow even further. Healing is something I do continuously with my clients because it is not a one-time process. You can and you will be more than capable of manifesting lovely juicy things without your healing and decluttering being 'complete'. Keep coming back to it and you will continue to attract more and more each time. Be gentle with your mind.

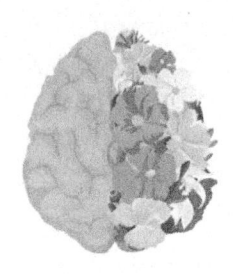

<u>Environmental Changes</u>

Our environment has a powerful influence on our thoughts, emotions, and behaviours. The people, places, and things we surround ourselves with can either support or hinder our progress towards our goals. That's why changing your environment can be a powerful tool for manifesting your desires and follows on nicely from step two.

You have already done the decluttering. This can help clear the way for new opportunities and positive energy to flow into your life. Next, we want to consider the people in your life. Surround yourself with supportive and positive individuals who believe in you and your goals. Distance yourself from negative people or 'energy vampires' who bring you down. This doesn't mean you have to cut people out of your life (unless you wish to), but it means protecting your energy and minimising these interactions where possible, or just taking a temporary time out.

One of the things I adore most about my client groups is the energy that the women bring in there. It is so empowering to be surrounded by likeminded souls who are all seeking growth and development. On that note, be sure to spend time in places that bring you joy and inspiration. Consider joining clubs, organisations, or societies that align with your values and interests.

I would also guide you to be intentional about the media you consume. Limit your exposure to negative news and focus on reading, watching, and listening to content that empowers and motivates you. I often swap the evening news for an inspiring podcast or *Dragons Den* instead. Be sure to clear out your social media too. Be selective on who and what you are exposing yourself too, especially if you are a bedtime scroller. The last thing we allow our brains to consume on an evening is what your subconscious will focus on as you sleep. Watching reruns of *Dexter* before bed is not ideal!

You can also make changes in your home environment to act as reminders and anchors of the life you are manifesting. Stick post it notes with your affirmations or intentions on the bathroom mirror; create a vision board; change your phone wallpaper to the holiday you want to take; update your computer password to the income you want to receive; and select crystals that are connected to your intention and keep them close by. See chapter 15 for more inspiration or even research some Feng Shui practices that can help cultivate an environment of wealth, love and joy.

Start to incorporate what I call incremental upgrades. If you are attracting wealth and success, what would you change in your home? It could be new bedding, posh coffee, getting the car washed or fresh flowers. You may go a step further and enjoy a hotel stay once a month or rent a luxurious office space for a week.

If you are manifesting love, do you have things in pairs around your home or do you just have the one wine glass? The bedside lamp on one side? The single bed? How does your underwear drawer make you feel? Would you let anyone else see those knickers? Give yourself permission to upgrade now. It can be with little things like fancy pyjamas, a new dinner set, even a leg wax!

The environment you create for yourself can either support or sabotage your efforts to manifest your desires. By making conscious choices about the people, places, and things in your life, the décor, fragrances and furtniture in your home, you can create a supportive and positive environment that helps you achieve your goals and also raises your vibration to match your intention.

In need of a quick manifestation boost? Move 27 items in your home. You don't need to get rid of them, just move them. Reorganising your belongings ushers in a fresh new energy so just wait and see what you manage to attract through this simple exercise.

What would you like to change in your environment?

How could you add incremental upgrades?

Do any particular colours or accessories align with your intentions?

Feel the Vibe & Avoid a Spiral

We already know, everything in the universe, including you, is energy. This energy vibrates at different frequencies and is what creates your reality. Understanding and recognising your energetic vibration is therefore one of the keys to manifesting your desires and living a fulfilling life.

The first part of the process in recognising your energetic vibration is to become aware of your thoughts and emotions. Your thoughts and emotions are the building blocks of your energetic vibration and play a significant role in determining the quality of your life experiences. Typically we dismiss or suppress these (thank you conditioning!) so this can be a learning curve for a lot of people who are used to switching off their feelings and emotions.

Take some time each day to reflect on your thoughts and emotions, even just a few minutes when you are waiting for the kettle to boil in the morning, or while you are brushing your teeth.

I use the following quick check ins:

How do I feel right now?
Where do I feel it in my body?
What are the thoughts running through my head?
Do I know why I am thinking and feeling this way?
Do I want to change it or enhance it?

Take note of any patterns or themes. This will give you a better understanding of your energetic vibration and what alters your frequency.

Some people are just naturally lower vibe when they first wake up but find a shift come lunch time. You will get used to your own patterns and then you will know when something is off that needs shifting.

Next, pay attention to how you react to situations and people. Do you often find yourself in negative or positive situations? This can give you an idea of the type of energy you are attracting into your life. Be mindful of your beliefs and limiting thoughts as well. This will also show you if you are immersed in the 3D or crossing the 4D bridge!

An exercise my clients LOVE (maybe not) is to write down every single negative thought, judgement, comparisonitus, conversation and situation for an entire week. (You see why they probably don't love this). It is time consuming, but it is a real eye opener. By writing them down, you take the charge out of it, (and switch off any triggered fight or flight response too) and you can then spot any of those patterns or themes. I use the notes app on my phone, but you could use your journal or even voice-note yourself.

Another step in my process is to employ **pattern interrupts** in these moments. Once you identify and acknowledge that a thought, feeling or situation is taking you into a dip or a place that is further away from your desire, you can interrupt it. I know a lot of couples do this during a disagreement too, so that they disperse the energy and come back to neutral, often using a random code word like *'banana'* to come out of the negative dip in an instant. I have had clients opt for star jumps when they feel their confidence nosedive and need an endorphine boost. Having a physical pattern interrupt is ideal because it will also relax your central nervous system.

An extreme example I have come across even involved eating dog food!! (These were not my clients, and I don't recommend this but hey, whatever works for you and takes you away from pain and towards pleasure!) You can also go deeper with these interrupts and use them as an energetic cleanse. Such as using emotional freedom technique (see below), a chord cutting meditation, sound bath or womb healing ceremony (see chapter 16), all of which will keep your nervous system chill and any fight or flight trigger switched off.

Please do not worry if you find you are at a pretty low vibration or that you can't be consistently high vibe. You are a human, and we know how cyclical we are (more on this later). Those low vibe times are ideal for figuring out what needs to change and making a plan. Those high vibe days are for enjoyment and living in the moment. We need both. Remember the Law of Polarity?

Witches are also noy afraid of the dark and we know there is great value in shadow work or connecting to the dark feminine as I do in my programmes. Of course, the higher your vibration, the more harmonious your life might be overall, but you are not expected to get there overnight, or to be in that state all the time. Imagine what an irritating, joyful, pain in the ass you would be if you were always a ray of sunshine! That is not the aim here; we aren't looking at creating robots. Progressing into your 5D quantum field is actually the most beneficial for your manifesting, but until you reach that point, working on your vibration can be a great booster. So I do want to show you how you can lift yourself to a neutral vibration or above when needed.

Here are some tips to help you raise your vibration up a notch or two:

- Practice gratitude: Taking time to appreciate the good things in your life can help you shift your focus away from negative thoughts and emotions. More on this in chapter 9.

- Engage in self-care: Engaging in activities that bring you joy, peace and fulfilment, such as exercise, meditation, or hobbies. Make a 'pleasure menu' of things that bring you an instant pick me up, that can be done anytime and aren't costly. You can then turn to your menu when you need that little boost and don't have the brain power to think of what to do. Just pick from your menu and do it.

- Surround yourself with good people: After all, your vibe attracts your tribe.

- Focus on the present moment: Worrying about the future or dwelling on the past can bring your vibration down. Focus on the present moment and appreciate what is happening now. The past has gone, so learn the lessons and let it go. Prepare for the future to ease your worries but trust the universe that you are in the right place right now.

- Choose your words carefully: The words you use can have a big impact on your vibration. Focus on speaking positively and avoid negative self-talk. Make a note of how you speak and even how you text – do you bring yourself down or talk about things that you don't want? Where your attention goes, energy flows.

- Practice positive thinking: Challenge those limiting beliefs and negativity you have identified that are holding you back and replace with positive affirmations or statements of intent. Even just *"I will be more positive today"* or *"I deserve my desires"* can be sufficient to stop you spiralling down a sad hole.

- Engage in acts of kindness: Doing good for others can help increase your vibration and bring more positivity into your life. Hello, Law of Karma!

- If your brain is in overdrive, write everything down or voice note it to yourself. Give your brain the space and dump it on to paper.

- Employ step five of my manifestation process and replicate the feelings behind your desires. How will you feel when you have achieved your intentions? When you move into your new home? Secure your promotion? Sign a new client? Go wedding dress shopping? Whatever feelings come up for you, how can you replicate them with another activity? Perhaps you would feel excited, so what else makes you excited? Maybe you would be proud or feel more confident, so what else gives you these feelings? It could be a day out at a theme park, looking through your certificates of achievement or wearing a new outfit. Anything that replicates the same feeling will shift your vibration to the same level, no matter how small. You might notice on some of my videos that I could be in sports wear (so nice and comfy) but wearing a bold lippy (to make me feel powerful and in my boss witch zone).

- Enjoy a meditation, some yoga or gentle stretches, stimulate your vagus nerve to support your nervous system, or have a go at my EFT tapping technique below.

EFT (Emotional Freedom Technique) is a self-help technique that involves tapping on specific points on the body to release negative emotions and physical pain. It is based on the principles of acupuncture and psychology and involves tapping on the meridian points of the body while focusing on a specific issue or emotion. The idea behind EFT is that negative emotions and physical pain can be alleviated by tapping on these meridian points and releasing the blockages that prevent the flow of energy through the body.

Some people find it helpful in reducing stress, anxiety and physical pain. Some studies have shown positive results for EFT in treating conditions such as anxiety and post-traumatic stress disorder (PTSD). I find it really soothing and often cough, cry or yawn- which is a great signal something has been released!

It's important to note that EFT tapping should not be used as a substitute for professional medical treatment. If you have a medical condition, it's always best to consult with a healthcare provider before trying EFT.

Step by step guide to EFT tapping:

1. Identify the feeling: Start by thinking about a specific feeling or emotion that you would like to release. It could be anything from stress, anxiety or sadness, to feeling exhausted or overwhelmed.

2. Rate the intensity: On a scale of 0 to 10, rate the intensity of the feeling you identified. This will help you measure your progress as you go through the tapping process.

3. Prepare the set-up statement: Say the set-up statement out loud, which will help you focus on the feeling and acknowledge it. The set-up statement should be in the form of: *"Even though I have this (insert feeling), I deeply and completely love and accept myself."* I encourage my clients to write several statements, based on all the negative thoughts or beliefs they are currently experiencing. As you tap, you can go through all of these statements.

4. Start tapping: Begin tapping with two fingers on the Karate Chop point on the side of your hand. Repeat the primary set-up statement three times as you tap to get you in the zone.

5. Tap on the points: Move onto tapping the points on your face, upper body and hands. These points are:

- Eyebrow
- Side of eye
- Under eye
- Under nose
- Chin
- Collarbone
- Under arm
- Top of head

6. Continue tapping: Continue tapping for 5-10 minutes or until you feel a noticeable shift in your energy and mood.

7. Rate the intensity: After tapping, rate the intensity of the feeling you identified earlier on a scale of 0 to 10. If the intensity has gone down, continue tapping until you reach a 0 if you can.

8. Add an affirmation or intention: To give you a boost alongside the releasing, as you tap on each point in the second round, repeat a positive affirmation or intention that resonates with you and the feeling you want to boost. For example, if you want to boost energy and mood, you could say, *"I am filled with positive energy and my mood is lifted"* or *"I intend to feel more positive and energetic today."*

9. Repeat as needed: Repeat this process as often as needed until you feel that your energy and mood have been boosted.

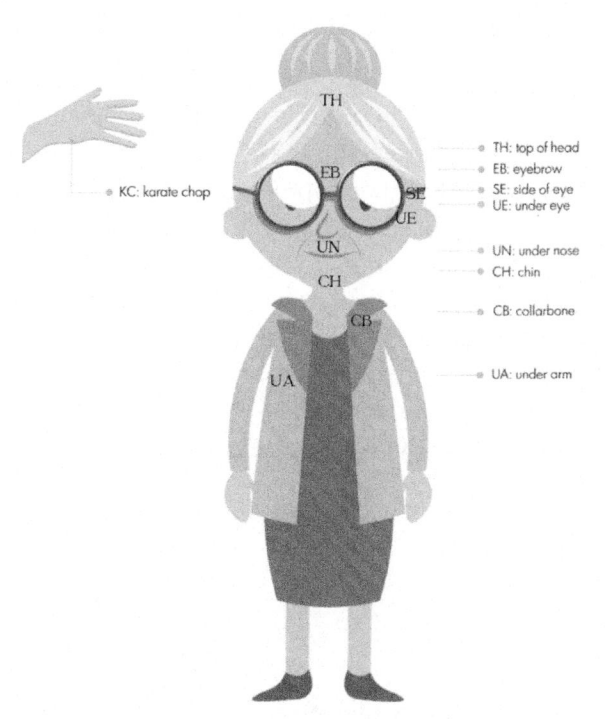

Please feel free to swap and change the tapping points to what feels good for you. It doesn't matter if you miss out a couple or forget the sequence or order. You can also add in fingertip taps, which is especially lovely if you are tapping on someone else or a child. There is also an extension to EFT which is amazeballs for shifting your thoughts and beliefs and creating a new narrative – called Matrix Reimprinting. You can train in this or study it further like I have, or you can simply read more about it for your own use. It is something I love to do in private sessions or on retreats, so if you enjoy tapping and want to advance further, check it out.

There are alternative practices to EFT that will also support your nervous system such as somatic healing, shamanic ceremonies and breathwork routines. The only one I don't particularly recommend for women is cold water swimming, only because this cools down your womb space, which as you will discover later is the portal for your manifesting and she likes to be warm!

As you work with these tools and start to be more mindful of your vibration, keep an eye out for any manifesting 'signals' and signs that pop up. You might keep seeing the car make and model that you are wanting to manifest. Or hear a particular song that you associate with your intention. If you connect to a spirit or power animal you might keep seeing them on cards or social media. All of these signs and signals is the universe showing you that you are on the same wavelength as your desire and vibrating at the same frequency. Keep going!

Expanders and Role Models

Manifesting your desires and living the life you want requires focus, determination, and effort (yay). This can get lonely, but there's also the fact that when things are taking longer than we would like, it can be demotivating, and we lose the belief that it is going to happen for us. This is why it can be super helpful to have support along the way to keep us going and also remind us that it is totally achievable to live the life that we want. That's where manifestation expanders and role models come in. Welcome to step six.

These wonderful beings have one or two roles. Firstly, they are there to support and encourage you with your manifestation efforts. These can be books, online resources, professional courses, or coaches and mentors who can help you gain new insights, perspectives, and techniques that can help you achieve your goals.

Secondly, they have the role of showing you the possibility. They are individuals who embody the qualities and characteristics you want to cultivate in yourself, or who already have what it is that you want. They can inspire and motivate you to take action and make positive changes in your life. Right now, I am surrounding myself in the online space and on my socials with authors, illustrators and publishers to get my vibe into the writing world and to show me that if they can do it, I can do it too. If you are reading this, hey, it worked and helped keep me going!

When looking for expanders and role models, it's important to choose people who are aligned with your values and goals. If you are looking to manifest wealth but your social media is full of B list celebrities who are blowing all their dollar bills on Botox and fillers and you don't agree with it, these aren't the expanders for you. As a side note, double check that your environmental declutter also included a thorough social media cleanse. Follow accounts that light you up and make you feel expanded, not contracted. Choose wisely.

Observing and learning from your expander's experiences and successes can also help you gain clarity and direction on your own path. If you are able to, spend time with these people or reach out and have a conversation. They may be happy to share how they got to where they are. If they have it, then it is possible for you too.

When I was single, I used to play the third wheel (or fifth, or seventh!) with my friends and their partners. Why would I put myself through such torture? Because I felt expanded in their presence and it was a loving reminder of how it feels to be in a relationship and that it was possible for me too. Please note, if you do not feel expanded around certain people or in certain circles then that is not the vibe for you. It may feel uncomfortable at first, sure, but if it ever feels really unpleasant, it will not be having the desired effect on your energy.

As an example, I have seen this happen with clients who have been trying for a baby and spent a lot of their time with their friends who were pregnant or had children already but found it to be so upsetting and more of a reminder of what they didn't have yet. They found it more beneficial to work on the decluttering elements and live in the moment of enjoying a child-free life. They have taken the bucket list holidays they wanted to do before they had children, whilst also indulging in quality food and experiences while they had the extra disposable income. The baby then did come along for most of these women, for those that it didn't, they had decided they preferred the nappy free way of living.

On a similar note, it is also helpful to have a support system of friends and family who believe in you and your goals. Surrounding yourself with positive and supportive people can help you stay motivated and focused on your manifestation efforts. Beware those energy vampires or people who let their ego speak up too often and put you down. Create your own super crew of cheerleaders or join a Tribe like mine where you are expanded and lifted every day.

Also be mindful of anyone in your circle who is triggering you as they reflect back your shadow side, that may give you signals of healing work or energetic cleansing that you need. *What are you projecting on to others?* Remember, **your perception, is a reflection, of your projection.** Sit with that one for a while…

Gratitude

Gratitude is the act of being thankful or showing appreciation for what you have in your life, regardless of its size or perceived significance. It naturally creates positive emotion and a higher energetic vibration that helps to shift us from dwelling on what's missing or wrong to what we have that is great in our life already.

Gratitude is important for manifesting because it helps to cultivate a positive and optimistic mindset, which in turn attracts more positivity and abundance. By focusing on what we are grateful for, we are signalling to the universe that we love what she has delivered and would like more of it please! I always say 'thank you' when paying a bill or handing over money to a cashier, so I signal to the universe to send me more money to spend. Before bed, I often ask Danny his favourite thing about the day so that we are in a state of gratitude before going to sleep (a great thing to do with your kids and partners too!) Of course, it also helps us feel better about ourselves and our circumstances, and often puts things into perspective too if we are having a crisis moment.

Practicing gratitude has been shown to improve physical and mental well-being, strengthen relationships, and increase resilience and overall happiness. So, in my book, it is well worth incorporating into your day.

Here are a few ways to practice gratitude:

- Keep a gratitude journal: Write down three to five things you are grateful for each day. This can help you focus on the positive aspects of your life and see how much you have to be thankful for.

- You could also write a mammoth list of *everything* you are thankful to have in your life and keep this as a reminder of how amazing your life is.

- Practice mindfulness: Pay attention to the present moment and focus on what you are grateful for in that moment. This can help you cultivate a deeper appreciation for life and the world around you, especially if you are having a moment when you are in a bit of a tizzy. Look at the things you can control and detach from those that you cant.

- Express gratitude to others: Let others know how much you appreciate them and what you are grateful for in your relationship with them. This can help strengthen your bonds and create positive energy in your relationships. Send a postcard or a little text, just to say thanks.

- Give back: Volunteer your time, money or resources to help others. This can help you cultivate a sense of gratitude for what you have and see the positive impact you can have on the world. This also meets one of our core human needs for fulfilment as we are making a contribution and doing something of significance.

- Reframe your thoughts: When faced with a challenge, try to see the positive side of the situation and focus on what you can learn or be grateful for. This can help you cultivate a more optimistic outlook on life. It can be tricky when the shit hits the fan to believe that it has happened for a reason. Trust me, I know! But it will be a lesson if nothing else, or a redirection to something better.

- Assign yourself a gratitude buddy: Somebody who you will text or call each day to share what you are thankful for. And they will do the same to you. Be prepared for the most positive text space you have ever seen!

- Use an anchor: Ever hear the story about the gratitude rock? A chap had a very poorly son who did not have a great prognosis. One day, he stumbled upon a small rock and decided to carry it around with him wherever he went. Every time he held the rock or felt it in his pocket, he gave thanks and appreciation for his son's health. Over time, it is believed his son recovered and they all lived happily ever after. I have no idea if it is a true story or a fable, but I love it either way. It serves as a reminder that gratitude and appreciation can have a profound impact on our lives. You could use a rock, a crystal, an item of jewellery, or even a photo or song. Something you will be in contact with often that will act as a reminder to give thanks.

- Witchy Bonus 1: Similar to our rock hero, focus on giving thanks for what you are wanting to manifest. His son did not have the best of health to begin with (an understatement!) but by giving thanks for what he wanted to manifest, the universe delivered more and more health to his son. We can all give thanks for things we don't have yet because we trust that they are on their way, and we can help speed it up. This can form part of your daily journal practice too.

- Witchy Bonus 2: Turn your anchor into an altar. You can have a sacred space in your home that is dedicated to your intentions and that acts as a constant reminder to give thanks for what is coming. We will talk about altars in more detail in chapter 13.

Gratitude is a habit that takes time and practice to develop so allow yourself to incorporate this in a way that feels good for you. By making it a regular part of your routine, helping yourself to remember with an anchor or stimulus, you can experience the many benefits it has to offer and speed up your manifestations at the same time.

What are you thankful for right now?

What anchor ideas do you have to remind you of how amazing your life is?

What are you grateful for that the universe is bringing to you?

GRATITUDE RITUAL

CLEANSE YOUR SPACE

Clear the area where you want to settle yourself. Smudge with Palo Santo or Sage if you wish and light your favourite smelling candle.

TAKE A BREATH.

Breathe in nice and deep through your nose to fill your lungs and let your tummy expand for 4 counts. Suspend the breath (not hold) for 4 counts, exhale through your nose for 4 counts and suspend again for 4 counts. Repeat 4 times.

THINK ABOUT YOUR DAY

What are you thankful has happened today, or if it is morning, what are you grateful you get to do today. What are you thankful to have in your life today. Let this fuzzy energy wash over you as you write these down.

WHAT ARE YOU MANIFESTING

Give thanks to your desires that you intend to receive and are already on their way to you. Thank the universe, God or your Goddess of choice for their love and support in bringing your desires in to fruition. Stay in this happy space as long as you wish. I like to pull an oracle card for some guidance too.

Manifesting vs Spellwork

Manifesting and spellwork are two different practices with different philosophies and approaches. However, they are both practices that involve harnessing energy and intention to bring about desired outcomes.

We know that manifesting is the idea that we create the reality we want by focusing our thoughts and energy on our desires. The universe then responds to these thoughts and feelings, so by focusing on what we want, we can attract it into our life. Tada!

Spellwork, is a form of magick that often involves using rituals, symbols and intention to bring about a desired outcome. Spellwork and witchcraft involve a more structured and intentional approach to manifesting, which means it is an epic way to enhance your existing manifestation practices. As I always say, spellwork is manifestation on heat!

You may have already tried working with affirmations or visualisation to align your energy with your desires. Witches do the same, but we also check for what other correspondences can support us too, for example, the moon phase, herbs and crystals. Chapter 15 is dedicated to magickal correspondences for you to learn about, so don't worry if this is new to you.

Both practices involve the use of energy and intention to bring about desired outcomes, and they share many similarities. They are both empowering practices that allow you to take control and co-create the reality you desire.

However, it is important to note that witchcraft is a spiritual practice that requires a certain level of knowledge, dedication, and respect for the nature, the Gods, Goddesses, the Ancestors and the Spirits. Which is exactly what you are learning in this book and what I teach in my programmes.

Now you have some of the basics and have a gorgeous (decluttered) foundation of gratitude and a high vibe mindset, let's bring in some magick…

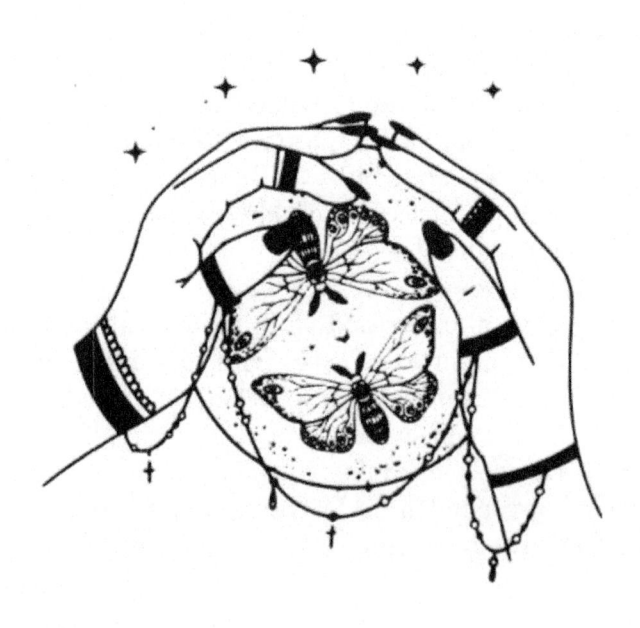

Grounding and Protection

Before we do any spiritual work, it is important to be personally prepared. This means being grounded, connected and protected so we are ready and clear to dedicate our space.

Grounding and protection are crucial steps before you start waving your wand around. These steps help to ensure that you are in the right state of mind and energy to perform your spell, as well as protecting yourself from any negative energy that may be present. If you are feeling unwell, or emotions are running high, you are angry, overwhelmed or upset, leave the spells until you feel in a better space. Remember, the intention that we put into our witchcraft will come back threefold. Even the seasoned witch will take a self-care break to approach her magick from a place of calm. Hectic energy brings hectic energy. Even if you are banishing negativity in your spells, we want to be zen AF when we do it. (As much as humanly possible).

Grounding is the process of connecting with the earth and bringing your energy back to a centred, balanced state. This is important because spellwork can be intense and emotional, and it can leave you feeling scattered or disoriented; another reason not to do it if you aren't feeling tip-top to begin with. Grounding helps you to focus your energy and to be fully present in the moment, which is essential for effective spellwork.

To ground yourself, you can try a few simple techniques such as:

1. Breathing: Yep, it is that simple. Take a few deep breaths, inhaling slowly and exhaling slowly, to calm your mind and focus your energy.

2. Visualisation: Visualise roots growing from the soles of your feet and connecting you to the earth. Imagine the roots sinking deep into the ground and absorbing the energy of the earth. This never fails to help me feel stable.

3. Physical connection: Stand barefoot on the ground or place your hands on the earth. This helps to physically connect you with the earth and to draw energy from it. Sit or lie down if it feels better.

I like to centre all my energy in my heart. I focus on unconditional love and send this love all the way down the body into my feet. I then visualise those roots of love and light going down into the centre of the earth and through the crystalline grid. The crystalline grid is like a big light multidimensional matrix that surrounds the planet and links to the crystals that we often find beneath the surface to make our lovely tumblestones, lamps and jewellery etc. The grid is also a memory store of human consciousness that remembers everything we do and where we do it. Ever get the feeling Mother Earth is pissed at the whole world? (Hello, natural disasters and pandemics!) She has accessed this information and repelled the negative energy right back where it came from. The grid has anchor points that are of a higher vibration across the planet, which creates major portals, vortexes and doorways to other dimensions. You may have visited some of these sacred sites, especially if you have been to any of the ancient wonders of the world, as our ancient ancestors were very aware of these vibrational peaks and portals. The Pyramids, Temples and Stone Circles are great examples.

You can send your love to Mother Earth and wrap your roots around the grid, which I like to imagine as a giant glowing clear quartz crystal, full of knowledge and linking us to the magick portals and the 5D world. You are now safe, protected and grounded from below. Draw this loving energy up from the Earth and into your heart.

I continue to send this love up through my body and out of the crown of my head to the universe, our creator and our celestial team. This attunes you to their love and guidance as you feel their love return to you. You are now safe and protected from above. Allow this love to fill your whole body.

Protection is the process of creating a barrier around yourself to protect you from any negative energy that may be present. Protection helps you to maintain a positive and safe environment for your spellwork and to avoid any unwanted interference. It's worth noting that this won't prevent other humans in your house from disturbing you, so I recommend crafting a sign asking them to politely bugger off for 10 minutes.

To protect yourself, you can try a few simple techniques such as:

1. Visualisation: Visualise a white light surrounding you, creating a protective shield. Imagine this light blocking out any negative energy and entities. I sometimes create a pink bubble for a bit of extra love.

2. Affirmations: Repeat affirmations such as *"I am protected"* or *"Only positive energy is allowed in my space."* These affirmations help to reinforce your intention and to create a protective barrier.

3. Herbs and crystals: You can also use herbs and crystals to enhance your protection. For example, black tourmaline is a powerful crystal for protection, and rosemary and salt are commonly used herbs for protection in spellwork, hence a circle of salt is often created. (Please don't try this if you have children or pets. The clean-up is also a real bastard!)

You may also like to ask your angels and guides for their protection as you visualise yourself in the white protective bubble, or you can invoke Archangel Michael. You can invite him to stand with you and see his cobalt blue light through and around you in every dimension. Ask him to protect your physical and etheric body, protecting you from both the inner and collective ego.

Remember to take your time with these steps and to focus on your intention, and you will be ready to perform your spellwork with confidence and success. Nothing scary will happen. No demons will pop up from the underworld and your house won't suddenly split in two. You are performing witchcraft not Hollywood CGI.

Deities and Goddesses

In many beliefs, Deities and Goddesses are spiritual beings or entities that are revered and worshiped. These Deities can be associated with specific aspects of nature, such as the Sun, Moon, Earth, or Sky. They can also be associated with human experiences, such as Love, Fertility, War, or Death. The exact nature of these Deities and the role they play varies greatly depending on the specific tradition or culture.

In some Pagan beliefs, such as Wicca, there is a belief in a dual deity system, with a God and a Goddess who are equal and complementary forces. In other traditions, such as Hinduism or ancient Greek mythology, there are many different Deities and Gods who are associated with various aspects of life and the natural world. One of the things I adore most about the witch's path, is you can honour, worship and call upon whichever Deity or Goddess you wish at any given time. Need a libido boost? Give the horned God a call. Looking for courage to make some bold ass moves? Freya is your girl. I have listed some of my favourite crew to call upon below.

The worship of these Deities and Goddesses often involves rituals, especially abound the Sabbats (our witchy holidays). We also provide offerings on our altars, and sometimes perform devotional practices that are designed to honour and connect with these spiritual beings. These rituals and practices can be performed alone or as part of a larger community, and they may involve the use of symbols, tools, and other objects that are associated with the Deity being worshiped.

Ultimately, the role of Deities and Goddesses can vary greatly, but they are often seen as powerful and influential forces that can provide guidance, support, and inspiration to those who seek to connect with them. It is quite nice for the solitary Witch to have some divine forces behind her work and someone to natter to.

As there are so many different Deities and Goddesses that can be called upon, I would encourage you to research and seek out your own list of favourites.

Some of my most commonly invoked Deities and Goddesses include:

- The Triple Goddess: This is a common Deity in Wiccan traditions and represents the three aspects of the feminine divine: the Maiden, the Mother, and the Crone. This is what I have tattooed on my wrist!

- The Horned God: A popular chap who represents the masculine divine, often associated with nature, fertility, and the hunt. Great for helping you take action.

- Aphrodite: The Greek Goddess of love, beauty, and sexuality. She is the Queen of desire and sexual energy and usually in the nuddy.

- Brigid: A Celtic Goddess associated with the hearth, home, and the arts. She is often our leading lady in the Sabbats and is connected to fire, healing and poetry.

- Diana: The Roman Goddess of the hunt, the Moon, and nature. She is a great Goddess to connect with in the wilderness and also for support during childbirth.

- Freya: A Norse Goddess associated with love, fertility, and war. Similar vibes to Aphrodite and Venus, but with warrior bad ass vibes. She also travels in a chariot pulled by cats, which is pretty awesome.

- Kali: A feisty Hindu Goddess associated with destruction and creation, power, and protection. She is your girl for supporting you with a total life overhaul and changing direction. She will literally obliterate anything in her way and was my homegirl during the pandemic!

- Osiris: An Egyptian God associated with death, the afterlife, and fertility. He is often called upon for support with agriculture, health and resurrection.

- Thor: A hammer wielding Norse God associated with thunder, strength, and protection who I obviously depict as Chris Hemsworth every time I think of him.

- Hecate: A Greek Goddess associated with magick, crossroads, and the underworld. She is often depicted holding two torches, with snakes or dogs, and is also associated with the three phases of the Moon, representing the Maiden, Mother, and Crone aspects of the Goddess. Hecate is commonly invoked in magick and ritual for protection, divination, and guidance as the Witches bestie.

- Venus: The Roman Goddess of love, beauty, and sexuality. She is a beautiful woman holding a mirror, symbolising her association with self-love and self-care. Venus is commonly invoked in rituals and spells related to love, relationships, and beauty, and is also associated with fertility and abundance.

- Lakshmi: A Hindu Goddess associated with wealth, prosperity, and good fortune. She is often seen holding a lotus flower and accompanied by elephants, and is considered to bring blessings of prosperity, abundance, and success.

- Shakti: A Hindu concept that refers to the feminine divine energy and power that underlies the universe. Shakti is often considered to be the divine mother, the source of all creation, and is deemed as the source of power and strength for all other deities.

- Father Sky: A Deity who represents the sky, the heavens, and the sun. This Deity is often associated with creation, light and life, and is sometimes seen as a source of all power and protection.

These are just a few examples of the many Deities and Goddesses that can be called upon in your rituals and spells. Your selection will depend on the purpose of the ritual or spell and your own preferences. Have a look at some of their images and see who you are most drawn to. It is also important to research their specific attributes and associated symbolism to ensure that you are calling upon the right Deity for your needs but, as with all of our magickal work, your intuition will know who you are best connecting with.

You can call on these legendary supporters in a variety of ways, depending on personal belief and practice. **Some common methods include:**

- Invocation: This involves speaking the name of the deity or goddess and asking for their presence and assistance during the spell or with a situation you are dealing with. Be sure when you ask for help from Kali or Hecate, as those babes take no prisoners. Remember, be careful what you wish for!

- Symbolism: Using symbols or items associated with the deity or goddess, such as candles, stones, or herbs, can help to evoke their energy and presence in the spell. You can pop these in your sacred space. (See next chapter).

- Visualisation: Visualising the deity or goddess in your mind's eye, and imagining their presence and energy in the space, can help to bring their essence into the spell. I often have a photo of them or change my phone wallpaper to their image if I need their energy a little longer term.

- Offerings: Making offerings such as food, drink, flowers, or incense, to show your respect and gratitude can help to establish a connection.

Not all practitioners of witchcraft believe in the existence of actual deities and goddesses. Some view them as archetypes or symbolic representations of certain energies or qualities. Regardless of personal belief, the act of calling upon them can still be a powerful tool. Remember to always thank them for helping you and let them get back to their own business when you are done.

Altars & Your Sacred Space

A witch's altar is a dedicated space used for ritual and spell work. It can be as simple or as elaborate as you wish, and may include items such as candles, crystals, herbs, symbols, and images of deities or spirits. You can have a permanent altar set up, such as on top of your dresser, fireplace or windowsill. Or a temporary altar may be more suitable for you if you have a busy household or are short on space. I have lots of mini altars around the house but for my spellwork and witchcraft, I have a temporary set up so I can move around as I wish. Having a nice storage box for your altar goodies also keeps their energy protected when not in use.

Your sacred space is simply your protected area for your spells, rituals and witchcraft. To create a sacred space, you can follow these steps or develop your own routine:

1. Cleanse the area: Physically clean the space, and energetically cleanse it with sage, salt (not with pets or sprogs), or other purifying substances. Palo Santo and sage are my favourites or a good old room spray.

2. Set your intention: Decide why you want to create a sacred space and what you hope to achieve in it. This will help you to focus your energy and create a clear purpose for the space. You can do this as you cleanse.

3. Choose your altar items: Choose items that resonate with you and that you feel will support your intention for the sacred space. This could include candles, crystals, herbs, symbols, etc. or traditional items such as an athame, cauldron or besom! (Broom)

4. You might bring in extra items that are specific to your particular spell, such as a photo of your chosen goddess or coloured paper and pens to write your wishes on.

5. Arrange your altar: Place your altar items in a way that feels aesthetically pleasing to you and that supports your intention for the space. You can do this based on directions if you wish (see information on elements in the next chapter).

6. Create a protective boundary: Cast a circle or create a protective boundary around the altar to symbolise the separation of the sacred space from the outside world. I usually do this in my mind as a visualisation but have also used crystals or rocks before too. I will then walk around the circle clockwise three times and call on the elements and the divine (see below).

7. Connect with the divine: Call upon the energies of the universe, the elements, the deity or deities of your choice, or any other source of spiritual energy you believe in to fill the space with their presence. As you face north, you can call upon the element of earth to bring grounding; facing east, you can call on the element or air to bring clarity; facing south, you can call upon the element of fire to bring energy; and facing west, you can call on the element of water to bring healing.

8. Begin your ritual or spell work: Use the altar and the sacred space to focus your energy, connect with the divine, and perform your ritual or spell.

Remember that the most important aspect of creating a sacred space is to focus your intention and connect with your personal power and the divine. The specific items and arrangements used on your altar will vary and there is no wrong way for you.

Elements

The five elements are a concept found in many spiritual and philosophical traditions. They are Earth, Air, Fire, Water, and Spirit (sometimes historically called Aether or Void). You are probably familiar with the pentagram symbol that you saw at the start of the book.... used for protection or banishing (depending on which direction you draw it).

This also represents the 5 elements witches connect with in our work.

We acknowledge these elements when we cast a circle before a spell (again for protection and as the official spell opening) as we often call on the guardians of each element and/or direction as we open the circle.

What you can also do, is have something to represent each element on your altar or sacred space (or simply the area where you do your woo woo and soulful practices).

I usually opt for:

- A photograph or statue of the Ancestor or Goddess I want to work with to represent Spirit. Your intention is also good enough for this. Just ask whatever spirit, guide or angel you wish to join you.

- Crystals, soil or salt to represent Earth. I have also been known to bring in a pot plant to my circles.

- Water is an easy one, just be sure to use a container that is only for your magickal purposes. Your favourite mug should be kept for your tea or coffee, and please don't give a wine glass used in a spell to a friend (unless you are trying to seduce them!) I also use seashells if water isn't convenient.

- For Air, I opt for incense (especially if the fragrance links to my intention, more on this in a later), a feather or athame (witches blade for inscribing on candles)

- Fire is another easy one - a candle, something red or a masculine influence. The Emperor or Sun Tarot cards are my go-to when I can't set things alight or a wand if I am feeling Harry Potter vibes.

As is the witch's way, there is no right and wrong. Even if you have none of these items, your desire to connect to the elements is enough. Working outside is also a great option or utilising crystals that represent each element is a nice alternative. Angelite is my favourite for air, Moss Agate for earth, Carnelian for fire and Aquamarine for water. Alternatively, Zeolite will represent them all.

Check the compass on your phone and place your earth goodies to the north; air goodies to the east; fire to the south; and water to the west. Spirit goes in the middle.

Outside of our sacred space, we witchies also like to work with the elements to feel more aligned with our manifestation intention and also to balance our energies if we are feeling too much of one element and not enough of another. Ever felt stuck? You want to have less earth 'mud' energy. Feeling overwhelmed with emotion? You need less water to avoid drowning. Also think about what happens when you combine each of the physical elements.

Mix earth and water = mud. Fire + air = more fire! Fire + water = no fire. Air + earth = balance. I encourage my clients to work with what I call the counter elements, when they are feeling too much of any one energy or not progressing as they would like to. This can show up especially around full moons or when we are in certain astrological signs.

Thinking about the energies that each element embodies can help you identify which element you need more or less of.

- Earth: Associated with stability, grounding, and manifestation in the physical realm. Using earth-based items such as stones, crystals, and herbs in spell work can help to bring stability and grounding to the manifestation process. Ideal if you want to bring your ideas in to fruition and bring yourself 'out of the clouds' a little. For working with Mama Earth and getting grounded, nothing beats being barefoot! Eating root veggies and having a digital detox can work wonders too.

- Air: Associated with communication, mental clarity, and new ideas. Using air-based items such as feathers, incense, and wind chimes in spell work can help to bring clarity and communication to the manifestation process. If you can't figure out what you want or what to do, you need some fresh air. As a double air sign, I feel my best when my brain is being worked to its highest capacity and I'm learning something new. Board games, breath-work and a windy mountain walk align me with this element nicely.

- Fire: Associated with passion, transformation, and manifestation of will. Using fire-based items such as candles, matches, and fire stones in spell work can help to bring passion and transformation to the manifestation process. It will also speed things up for you if you need a bit of a kick up the bum and extra dose of motivation. When I need that fire, it's got to be working out and hitting the gym for me. Surrounding myself with candles or toasting marshmallows on a campfire comes a close second.

- Water: Associated with emotions, intuition, and manifestation of the subconscious. Using water-based items such as seashells, clear quartz, and water in spell work can help to bring emotional balance and intuition to the manifestation process. It is also highly cleansing and gives you a fresh start. I am a real water baby which is surprising as I have zero water signs in my astrological chart, but I love being in and around water. Of course, I am a Mama Moon lover (see the moon chapter for working with her) and I really enjoy creative activities and dreamwork to connect with this element too. But, by far the easiest way to align with water.... drink it!

- Spirit: Associated with connection to the divine, higher self, and manifestation of spiritual desires. Using items that symbolise spirit such as a clear quartz crystal or a visual representation of the divine can help to bring spiritual energy and connection to the manifestation process. It's also a huge comforter and reassurance that you are supported.

Use these ideas for inspiration and see how you get on with connecting to these nature elements. They all bring a different medicine.

Earth   Water   Fire   Air   Ether

Magickal Correspondences

Witchcraft correspondences refer to the concept that various elements in the natural world, such as plants, minerals, animals, and celestial bodies, can correspond to specific energies, qualities, and powers that can be invoked or utilised in our magick and ritual practices to give them a little something extra (and make us feel super cool with our apothecary of goodies).

In both traditional and modern day witchcraft, different systems of correspondences have been developed that associate specific herbs, crystals, tarot cards, planetary energies, and other elements with particular magickal properties, such as protection, love, divination, or banishing negativity. These correspondences can be used to create spells, charms, talismans, and other magickal tools, or to inform the timing and focus of rituals if you wish.

For example, a spell for protection might involve using herbs like rosemary, mint, and frankincense, which are associated with protection and purification, along with crystals like black tourmaline or obsidian, which are known for their grounding and protective qualities. Similarly, a spell for love might include ingredients like rose petals, cinnamon, and vanilla, which are linked to love and attraction, and may be performed during the Waxing Moon, when the energy of growth and manifestation is strongest.

Witchcraft correspondences are not fixed and can vary between different cultures and traditions. Some of us create our own correspondences based on personal experience and intuition, while others follow established systems handed down through their lineage or tradition. Unless you are following a specific tradition, I would allow yourself the freedom to take all of these correspondences as ideas and inspiration, but to ultimately trust your own instincts and desires of what you like to work with. I love working with moon phases, colours, crystals, scents and herbs, but rarely account for the time of day and planetary alignment. Have fun seeing what you enjoy best. It should never feel like a chore to be creating and crafting your spells and rituals, rather it should be an enhancement to your manifesting and make you feel good.

Colours

Colours can be incorporated into spellwork in various ways, such as through candles, cloths, or crystals. I like to use corresponding coloured pen and paper or create a spell bag or pouch in the corresponding colour. Think about what it is you want to manifest and check which colours are going to give you that boost. Even wear that colour if you can!

Red is associated with energy, passion, love, and strength. It can be used in spells to increase physical energy, attract love and passion, or to increase courage. Also connected to the root chakra and stability.

Orange is associated with creativity, joy, and confidence. It can be used in spells to increase happiness and confidence, stimulate creativity, or attract success.
Also connected to the sacral chakra and passion.

Yellow is associated with mental clarity, communication, and intelligence. It can be used in spells to increase self-esteem, stimulate communication, or enhance mental clarity and focus. Also connected to the solar plexus and confidence.

Green is associated with growth, healing, abundance, and fertility. It can be used in spells to promote physical healing, attract abundance and prosperity, or to increase fertility.
Also connected to the heart and happiness.

Blue is associated with peace, tranquility, and intuition. It can be used in spells to promote peace and calm, enhance communication and self-expression, or increase intuition and psychic abilities. Also connected to the throat chakra.

Purple is associated with spirituality, psychic ability, and manifestation. It can be used in spells to increase spiritual growth, enhance psychic abilities, or to attract manifestation and success. Also connected to the third eye.

Pink is associated with love, friendship, and emotional healing. It can be used in spells to attract love, improve relationships, or to promote emotional healing.

Brown is associated with stability, grounding, and protection. It can be used in spells to increase stability, ground energy, or to provide protection.

Black is associated with banishing negativity, protection, and releasing energies. It can be used in spells to banish negativity, provide protection, or to release negative emotions and energies.

White is associated with purity, clarity, and protection. It can be used in spells to purify and cleanse energy, increase clarity, or to provide protection. Also sometimes connected to the crown chakra.

Herbs and Plants

Herbs have been used in witchcraft, plant medicine and other forms of magick for centuries, as they are believed to possess a wide range of energies and properties that can be harnessed for various purposes. You can, of course, cook with certain herbs, add them to your morning tea, or sprinkle them during your spells. I quite like to make herb pillow pouches (in a corresponding colour pouch, of course) that help boost my manifestations while I sleep. Be sure to use different tools when preparing your herbs for magick rather than your regular kitchen utensils. Objects store energy and we want to keep our magickal tools as clear as we can.

Rose: Associated with love, friendship, and emotional healing. It can be used in spells to attract love and friendship, or to promote self-love, beauty and balance.

Lavender: Bringing peace, protection, and a good night's sleep. It can be used in spells to promote relaxation and calm, or to provide protection whilst you are in the land of nod.

Mint: Cultivating energy, protection, and purification. It can be used in spells to increase motivation, provide safety and boundaries, or purify energy and spaces.

Cinnamon: Attracting love, prosperity, and energy. It can be used in spells to attract romance, increase wealth, or to give you a nice boost of luck.

Sage: Often used for cleansing, purification, and wisdom. It can be used in spells to increase wisdom and knowledge, or to cleanse and banish negative energy.

Thyme: Not just for a roast dinner, Thyme gives us courage, protection, and healing. It can be used in spells for health, wellbeing and confidence.

Alfalfa: Often used for health, prosperity, and good luck. It can be used in spells to attract money, protect your home and assets, and bring good health.

Basil: Another great money maker and also used for purification and love. Basil can be used in spells for prosperity, healing and attracting romance.

Rosemary: Ideal for the kitchen witch looking for extra strength, love and healing. Can be used in cooking or spells for purification and clarity. I also have a pot of rosemary by the front door for protection.

Mugwort: Always feels magickal to me. It's a herb for psychic development and witches intuition. It can be used in spells or divination work when you are seeking clarity and direction. (Toxic in essential oil form so be careful – I always opt for dried)

There are many other herbs that can be used in witchcraft, each with its own unique properties and energies. Some witches also use flowers, roots, seeds, or other plant parts in their spells and rituals.

You may also find these herbs used in fragrances and scents that you can also utilise in your practice and to lift the vibration of your space. (See other ideas below).

While herbs can be powerful tools in magick and spellwork, they should be used with caution and respect. Some herbs may have toxic or harmful effects if used improperly, so it's important to research the properties of each herb before using it and be sure you don't have an allergy or any peckish pets strolling around. Additionally, I always like to consider the ethical implications of using plant materials in magick, and to source herbs from sustainable and responsible sources whenever possible.

Fragrances/ Scents

Scents and fragrances can play an important role as they are believed to have the ability to alter mood and energy, as well as enhancing intention and focus. Ever feel lost without a spritz of your favourite perfume? Felt your mood lift when you walked into a nice smelling room? Or felt it dip when your house smells of old socks? This is a powerful and easy to implement magickal tool that most of us have already been doing for years.

Some of my favourites are:

- Sandalwood: Can be used to ground energy, provide protection, or to facilitate spiritual growth.

- Orange: Associated with happiness, abundance, and manifestation. This is an instant mood lifter.

- Patchouli: For feminine energy, love, friendship, and healing. A very 1960's hippie fragrance that is one of the most common incense purchases.

- Frankincense: Often associated with spirituality, protection, and purification. It can be used to increase spiritual connection and psychic abilities, provide strength, or to cleanse energy and spaces (it can be very smokey as an incense so open a window).

- Jasmine: The ultimate aphrodisiac (oo-err!). Associated with love, sex, dreams and emotions. I love this one as an oil in my bath or in a nice cup of tea.

- Bergamot: My favourite for stress release and reducing anxiety. It is also great to use for house magick and cleansing.

- Ylang Ylang: Another love cultivator and sexy minx. Also great for confidence and boosting your mood. This is a go to scent for those first dates.

- Vanilla: A comforting smell that always reminds me of cake. It raises your energy as well as bringing positivity into your home and heart. Vanilla candles will make your home feel like a safe sanctuary in no time.

- Black Pepper: Our banishing friend to keep negative energy (and people) away. It also relaxes the nervous system and is great for digestive problems. Just use in small doses.
- Tea Tree: I am not actually a fan of the smell and seem to have a reaction with pure tea tree oil, however this is the best oil for a reset after being poorly or to rid your space of any negativity. Think of it as a reset and transform scent.

You can choose to use essential oils, incense, candles, or other fragrant materials in your spells and rituals. You can also create personalised blends or creams based on your intentions and desires. I always pick up a hand created fragrance or two when I am visiting witchy fairs and festivals to spritz around my home or for my healing circles.

Again, be sure to check for sensitivities or allergies to certain fragrances before spritzing yourself and others.

If you have oils, you can dot them on your pulse points, breath them in, or add to your bath or shower. I like to blend them in to a cream or add to a carrier oil such as almond or grape-seed oil to use like a lotion. Using incense or a diffuser is great for filling your space with the desired intention as well as being super relaxing. (Watch a back flow incense burner and you will be mesmerised!)

Crystals

Whether you want to build up a tumble stone collection to pop in your bra; enjoy the power from pyramid and tower crystals; carry a worry stone; or wear some fabulous crystal jewellery, here are some of the key crystal players in the manifestation game:

- Clear Quartz: The master healer, associated with clarity, amplification, and healing. Clear Quartz is also a stand in for when you don't have a particular crystal, for it will cultivate whatever energy is required for the intention you desire. It is also a good office energiser.

- Amethyst: For spirituality, psychic development, protection, and emotional balance. This is the stone for healers and students. Helping with memory and focus as well as dream recall, this is a good bedtime buddy. Also handy in the kitchen if you are prone to stress eating!

- Citrine: The money stone. Used for attracting abundance, prosperity, and manifestation. Pop this little dose of sunshine in your purse or wallet.

- Carnelian: The success stimulator. Carnelian is associated with courage, motivation, and creativity as well as your womb space and sacral chakra. I like to wear this one as a power boost during menstruation or if I am doing any public speaking.

- Rose Quartz: The love stone for romance, friendship, and emotional healing. Great for your heart chakra but also for regulating the energy in your whole body.

Pop a piece of rose quartz in your bathroom or the room on the far right as you enter your home. This will help any visitors feel at ease and comfortable in your space.

- Red Jasper: Commonly associated with grounding, stability, and strength. It is believed to have a stabilising effect on the body and is my favourite to balance the root chakra, which is associated with survival, safety, and security. Red Jasper is also believed to promote physical vitality and stamina and can be useful in providing support during times of stress or when facing challenges. Additionally, it is said to enhance creativity, focus, and determination, making it a popular stone for artists, writers, and entrepreneurs.

- Black Tourmaline: (or any other black crystal) Will bring protection, grounding, and protection against negative energy and influences. It also removes pain, heartbreak and illness. Pop this in your hallway or living room.

- Labradorite: Connecting to your intuition, and spiritual growth, this is a favourite for witches and mystics. It also helps cleanse your aura and clear your mind if it is a little overwhelmed.

- Pyrite: Or 'Fool's Gold' thanks to its gold and shiny appearance. This is another abundance and prosperity stone as well as being used for confidence and protection. Keep this one in the front window of your home.

- Tigers Eye: For courage and protecting your energy. This is a good luck crystal that also reminds you of your inner (tiger) strength.

- Aventurine: A general healing stone and heart opener. This is my favourite for overall wellbeing and ideal for any fellow overthinkers. It brings you back to your centre and out of your head.

You may also choose to use specific crystals based on your personal experiences or based on the energies and properties associated with specific zodiac signs, your chakras, or just whichever crystal tickles your pickle that day. Visit a crystal shop if you can and just allow yourself to be drawn to whatever crystal wants to be with you.

Always handle and care for your crystals with respect, and cleanse and charge them regularly to maintain their energetic properties. I simply pop mine on the windowsill under the Full Moon or waft them through some Palo Santo or sage smoke. Be careful of putting them in water – some are soluble!

Astrological signs

We know that astrological signs each have their own personality traits so we can tap into these qualities and attributes to enhance our magick and manifesting. You can utilise these energies by performing your spells or rituals when the Sun is in this particular sign (keep in mind this is only for one season a year) or as the Moon passes through this sign (which typically happens at some point every month). Check on a Moon calendar or app for the dates based on the current year and your geographical location.

Aries: Courage, action, and leadership.

Taurus: Abundance, sensuality, and stability.

Gemini: Communication, intelligence, and adaptability.

Cancer: Emotions, nurturing, and protection.

Leo: Creativity, confidence, and stepping up.

Virgo: Practicality, organisation, and healing.

Libra: Balance, relationships, and diplomacy.

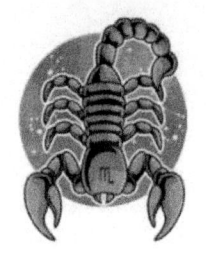

Scorpio: Transformation, sexuality, and power.

Sagittarius: Adventure, optimism, and growth.

Capricorn: Discipline, stability, and structure.

Aquarius: Innovation, independence, and humanitarianism.

Pisces: Intuition, spirituality, and compassion.

Planets

Similar to the astrological signs, you can also check what the planets are up to at the time of your spell or work with their energy on the corresponding day of the week. After all, the ancient Romans named the days of the week after their Gods and planets, and this system of naming was later adopted by the Germanic and Norse cultures. For example, the name for Saturday comes from the Roman God Saturn, and the name for Sunday comes from the Sun.

- Sun: Vitality, leadership, and personal power.
- Moon: Emotions, intuition, and change.
- Mercury: Communication, intelligence, and travel.
- Venus: Love, relationships, and beauty.
- Mars: Courage, action, and sexuality.
- Jupiter: Abundance, growth, and expansion.
- Saturn: Discipline, stability, and structure.
- Uranus: Innovation, change, and rebellion.
- Neptune: Spirituality, creativity, and dreams.
- Pluto: Transformation, power, and control.

Days

The days of the week originated in paganism as a way to organise time and connect with the natural world and its cycles. These pagan cultures saw the days of the week as a tool to connect with the divine and to bring blessings and protection. They would often perform rituals to the corresponding deity for each day, as a method of harnessing their power.

Today, we tend to use the days of the week to align with specific energies and focus our intention in spells and rituals.

The correspondences for each day of the week have evolved over time, but they still hold much of the same significance as they did in ancient pagan cultures. If it doesn't fit with your schedule, if the Moon is not in the desired phase or there is a retrograde going on, don't worry. Your intention is the strongest tool of all. Your magick is meant to work for you and that means it has to fit around your life, not the other way around.

- Monday: Corresponds with the Moon, symbolising intuition, emotions, and subconscious mind.
- Tuesday: Corresponds with Mars, symbolising energy, passion, and courage.
- Wednesday: Corresponds with Mercury, symbolising communication, intellect, and adaptability.
- Thursday: Corresponds with Jupiter, symbolising growth, abundance, and good fortune.
- Friday: Corresponds with Venus, symbolising love, relationships, and beauty.
- Saturday: Corresponds with Saturn, symbolising discipline, stability, and structure.
- Sunday: Corresponds with the Sun, symbolising success, confidence, and personal power.

Numbers

Numerology can be used as a tool to enhance your spells by writing your intention a particular number of times, repeating affirmations that have a certain number of words, or by inscribing numbers on to your spell candle or as part of a sigil.

You may have also heard of 'angel numbers' referring to repeating sequences of numbers that are believed to hold special significance and guidance from Angels. I tend to price all of my offerings based around these numbers too!

1: Represents new beginnings, independence, and leadership. It is often associated with the element of Fire and the tarot card The Magician.

2: Represents balance, harmony, and duality. It is often associated with the element of Water and the tarot card The High Priestess.

3: Represents creativity, growth, and communication. It is often associated with the element of Air and the tarot card The Empress.

4: Represents stability, grounding, and material manifestation. It is often associated with the element of Earth and the tarot card The Emperor.

5: Represents change, transformation, and growth. It is often associated with the element of Fire and the tarot card The Hierophant.

6: Represents love, harmony, and balance. It is often associated with the element of Water and the tarot card The Lovers.

7: Represents spirituality, intuition, and inner wisdom. It is often associated with the element of Air and the tarot card The Chariot.

8: Represents abundance, success, and material wealth. It is often associated with the element of Earth and the tarot card Strength.

9: Represents completion, fulfilment, and spiritual attainment. It is often associated with the element of Fire and the tarot card The Hermit.

10: Represents completion, wholeness, and the end of a cycle. It is often associated with the element of Earth and the tarot card The Wheel of Fortune.

11: Considered a master number in numerology, 11 represents intuition, spiritual awakening, and enlightenment. It is often associated with the element of Air and the tarot card Justice.

12: Represents harmony, balance, and the union of opposites. It is often associated with the element of Water and the tarot card The Hanged Man.

13: Often considered an unlucky number in Western culture, 13 actually represents transformation, death and rebirth, and the Goddess. It is often associated with the element of Fire and the tarot card Death.

14: Represents stability, grounding, and the practical manifestation of goals. It is often associated with the element of Earth and the tarot card Temperance.

15: Represents change, growth, and the manifestation of new opportunities. It is often associated with the element of Air and the tarot card The Devil.

16: Represents spiritual growth, revelation, and transcendence. It is often associated with the element of Water and the tarot card The Tower.

17: Represents ambition, leadership, and the ability to manifest one's desires. It is often associated with the element of Fire and the tarot card The Star.

18: Represents manifestation, abundance, and material success. It is often associated with the element of Earth and the tarot card The Moon.

19: Represents transformation, new beginnings, and the integration of the spiritual and physical. It is often associated with the element of Air and the tarot card The Sun.

20: Represents balance, harmony, and the union of the spiritual and physical. It is often associated with the element of Water and the tarot card Judgment.

These correspondences can be used in a variety of ways in spells and rituals that align with your intention, or performing spells on specific days of the week or Moon phases that are connected with the desired outcome (see next chapter). It's important to note that correspondences are not set in stone and can vary based on individual beliefs and practices. Feel free to create your own and trust your intuition on what to include in your magick.

As always, everything we utilise should be used with respect and caution, and never to harm others. If you gather herbs and flowers from Mother Nature's garden, be sure to thank her. The most powerful item in our toolkit is always our intention and that is the only thing you need. Everything else is just a bonus.

What inspiration or ideas have popped up for you after reading about correspondences?

Write down any correspondences that you feel drawn to incorporate in to your spells and rituals

Moon Phases and Rituals

Moon phases can have a significant impact on magick and manifestation, as the energy and influence of the Moon can amplify and direct the intentions set during rituals and spells. Here's a rundown of the different Moon phases and their general correspondences for spells and manifestation:

- New Moon: A New Moon occurs when the Moon is not visible in the sky, as it is positioned between the Sun and the Earth. It is a time of new beginnings, fresh starts, and setting intentions. This is an ideal time to start new projects, set goals, and focus on self-improvement.

- Waxing Crescent: During this phase, the Moon is growing and becoming more visible each night. It is a time of growth, expansion, and manifestation. This is a good time to cast spells for personal growth, increasing prosperity, and attracting new opportunities.

- First Quarter: The first quarter occurs when half of the Moon is visible and is positioned at a right angle to the Sun. This is a time of conflict, challenges, and decision-making. This can be a good time to focus on making difficult decisions, letting go of negative energy, and finding solutions to problems.

- Waxing Gibbous: During this phase, the Moon is getting fuller and brighter each night. It is a time of abundance, manifestation, and bringing your desires to fruition. This is a good time for spells and rituals related to abundance, prosperity, and success.

- Full Moon: A Full Moon occurs when the Moon is fully visible in the sky and is positioned opposite the Sun. It is a time of manifestation, fruition, and release. This is a powerful time to cast spells for abundance, manifestation, and releasing negative energy.

- Waning Gibbous: During this phase, the Moon is getting smaller and less bright each night. It is a time of letting go, releasing, and closure. This is a good time for spells and rituals related to letting go of negative energy, breaking negative patterns, and closing chapters in your life.

- Third Quarter: The third quarter occurs when half of the Moon is visible and is positioned at a right angle to the Sun. This is a time of reflection, contemplation, and inner wisdom. This is a good time for spells and rituals related to self-reflection, spiritual growth, and finding inner peace.

- Waning Crescent: During this phase, the Moon is becoming smaller and less visible each night. It is a time of endings, release, and closure. This is a good time for spells and rituals related to letting go of negative patterns, releasing negative energy, and closing chapters in your life. The prime time for shadow work and connecting to your dark feminine.

Rituals

I also love working with the Moon through rituals. If you are new to working with the Lunar Cycle and the magick of Mama Moon, I would focus on the New and Full Moons. Once you are ready to progress, you can check in with the first and last quarters before encompassing the Waxing and Waning Moons into your practices too. I like to see them as a weekly or fortnightly check in with yourself, even for just 10 minutes to see if your manifestations and intentions are on track or need a bit of attention. This really helps us work in conjunction with divine timing too, rather than projecting our intentions out in to the distant future (e.g. 'I wish to be a size X by next Christmas, guarantees you won't achieve that goal until 'next Christmas' which is a moment in time that is always in the future, never in the present...) By working with monthly, fortnightly or weekly rituals, it is part of your manifesting routine that keeps you focused on just one lunar cycle.

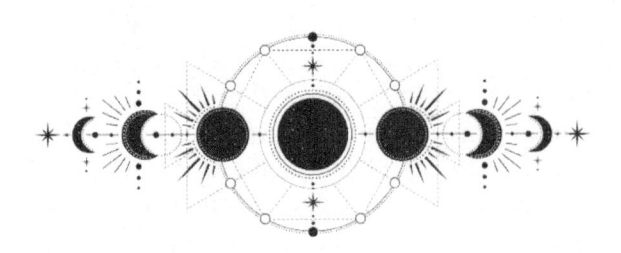

New Moon

The New Moon is the beginning of a brand-new cycle as the Sun, Moon and Earth are all in alignment. This is when you can take any discoveries you have uncovered about what you don't want and transform them into what you do want.

You want to visualise and imagine all of your dreams and desires, and set your intentions how you could show up and co create with the universe to get there.

This is a time for making plans and planting the seeds to bring to life. Be creative, and gain clarity on what you want to manifest. You might like to create a vision board or use affirmations. Think about areas of your life that need attention, what you want to achieve throughout the next lunar cycle and what you are manifesting.

- Have a cleansing ceremony with Palo Santo or Sage to smudge your home and clear the environment – really let the smoke get into those corners of the room. Frankincense oil can be used to cleanse your aura - just rub a few drops between your palms, enjoy the fragrance and then run your hands over the outside of your body.

- Think about what has shifted for you since the last Full Moon - *Have you let go of anything?*

What emotions have you experienced over the last few days?

- *Make a list of people, situations and things that you are thankful for.* Send love to anyone you have written on your list.

- Decide what you want to create in the next lunar cycle and *make a wish list.* I tend to aim for 3 – 4 things.

- Really focus on each of your wishes and what exactly you want to manifest but most importantly how it would make you feel. *Are there any activities that replicate these feelings that you can incorporate into your day?*

- Meditate and visualise these wishes coming true and enjoy the emotions that come with it. You might like to do this daily.

- *Create some affirmations* to anchor you to your wishes coming true. Try to think of three to use for the Waxing Moon phase. Choose statements of intent if it feels better.

- What *three actions* will you take to move towards your dreams within the next 7 days?

Full Moon

The Full Moon is the climax of the lunar cycle. No need to worry if you feel a bit 'loony' around the Full Moon. It is caused by the build-up of energy, as well as everything coming to its peak and being highlighted by Mama Moon. This is a great time to journal about your dreams and make a note of any negative thought patterns or other aspects that may be showing themselves under the moonlight just now.

It is also a good time to release those lower vibrations and energies which no longer serve us. The time to wipe the slate clean and look within, reflect, heal and shift those blocks.

In order to receive we have to release. Which is where the forgiveness and gratitude practices come in to allow our manifestations the space to come through. The Full Moon energy helps us to process and let go. It is often when our manifestations come into fruition.

- Have a cleansing ceremony as you would for the New Moon.

- *What are the main emotions you have been experiencing in the run up to this Full Moon? What does this tell you or signal for you to change or embrace?*

- *What has changed for you since the last New Moon? Are your goals still the same for this month?*

- *What is getting in your way or proving challenging?* (This is what you need to shine a light on and release or overcome if you can)

- *What actions can you take during the Waning Moon to remove things in your way?*

- *What are your three Waning Moon affirmations?*

- You can also have a burning ceremony if it is safe to do so, or a water ceremony - write each thing you wish to release on separate pieces of paper. Hold each piece to your heart and say what you wish to release, before setting it alight and dropping it into a fireproof dish (or for no fire involvement, simply drop it in to a bowl of water – perhaps with a floating candle on top!) You can then leave the dish/bowl out under the moonlight until the next morning.

Lunar Boosters

Crystals will help amplify your intentions. Moonstone is a great choice for bringing the energy of the Moon to you and Clear Quartz will amplify your intentions.

A Moon altar can be a lovely sacred space to perform your Moon rituals. You may have candles, crystals or Moon related goodies.

Taking a Moon bath (or shower) beforehand will help connect you to and draw on the Moon energies. This can be outside as a visualisation exercise of the Moon bathing you, or you can take a physical bath. You could also add some Epsom salts, aromatherapy oils, flower petals and light some candles.

Moon candles can help with sending out your intentions. Having a different candle for a Full Moon and New Moon can be a nice touch. They don't need to be expensive, just a regular pillar candle will do. You can work with your candle when you are making Moon wishes and repeat this daily throughout the lunar cycle if you wish.

What are your favourite ways to honour the moon phases?

Menstruation Magick, Womb Wisdom & Sexual Power

The Moon and Menstruation (one for the ladies)

The connection between the Moon phases and the menstrual cycle has long been recognised in many cultures, as both are cyclical and have similar rhythms. Some witchies (me included) believe that the menstrual cycle can have a significant impact on the power and effectiveness of spellwork and manifestation. We feel differently at each stage of our cycle, whether we bleed or not, or whether we have hormonal contraception or not. Our energy, vibe and mood totally change week by week and day by day. We don't have a 24-hour cycle like men, we have a 28-day (ish) cycle like the Moon, regardless of if we have a physical womb or not.

The exact timing for when magick and witchcraft is most powerful during a woman's menstrual cycle will vary depending on your own body. I always advise my clients to track their energy, feelings and emotions over 1 – 2 months so they can start to spot the patterns. You can then work with this to tailor your nutrition, exercise, business acitivies and social plans too!

As a typical idea, this is what most of us will experience. But of course, every cycle can be different too:

- Menstruation: This time is often associated with letting go of old energy, purification, and renewal.

It can be a good time for self-care, inner reflection, and releasing negative patterns. During this time, you may prefer to focus on you, your self-love, and renewal, rather than actively casting spells or engaging in manifestation practices. This time can also be used for spells related to letting go of negative patterns, releasing old energy, and preparing for new growth. I also find my divination powers to be strongest at this time, so it is ideal for card readings.

- Follicular phase (from the start of menstruation to ovulation): This is a time of growth, manifestation intentions, and new beginnings. It can be a good time for setting goals, starting new projects, and focusing on personal growth. You might like to cast spells and engage in manifestation practices related to new endeavours, growth, and development. The energy of this phase is said to be more open and receptive, making it ideal for attracting positive changes and opportunities.

- Ovulation: This is a time of peak fertility, abundance, and luck. It can be a good time for spells related to money, prosperity, and attracting new opportunities or people. This is a time of increased energy and is also believed to be a good time for spells related to attracting love, passion, and physical well-being. We are our most physically attractive during this stage after all!

- Luteal phase (from ovulation to the start of menstruation): This is a time of reflection, inner wisdom, and closure. It can be a good time for spells related to self-reflection, spiritual growth, and finding inner peace.

The energy of this phase is said to be more introspective, making it ideal for work related to exploring one's inner self and discovering deeper truths.

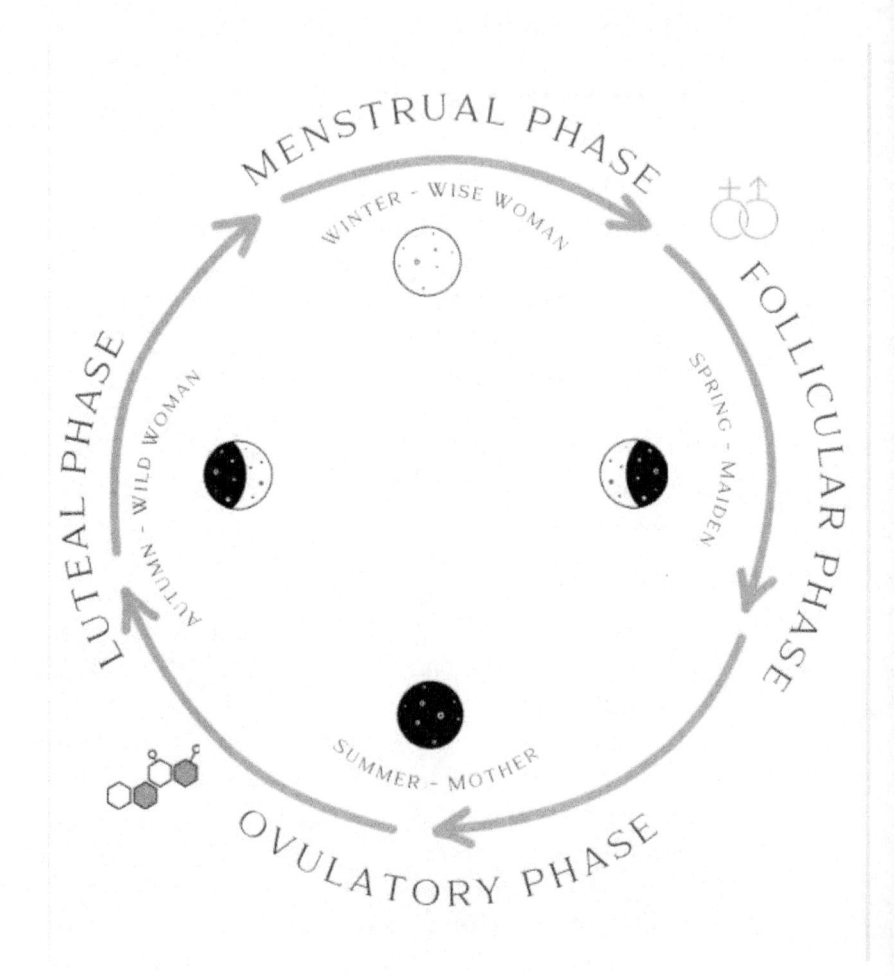

Certain Goddesses are also associated with the different phases of the menstrual cycle. This connection is based on the idea that the phases of the menstrual cycle reflect the natural cycles of growth, change, and renewal that occur in the physical world and in the lives of women.

- Menstruation: This phase is associated with the Wise Woman or the Goddess Lilith, who is often portrayed as a powerful and independent Goddess who represents the wise yet untamed feminine energy. During this phase, women may choose to connect with Lilith to release negative patterns, let go of old energy, and purify their bodies and spirits.

- Follicular phase: This phase is associated with the Maiden or Goddess Athena, who represents youth, courage, and determination. During this phase, women may choose to connect with Athena to gain clarity, focus, and motivation in pursuit of their goals.

- Ovulation: This phase is associated with the Mother or Goddess Aphrodite, who represents love, beauty, and passion. During this phase, women may choose to connect with Aphrodite to cultivate love and compassion for themselves and others, and to tap into their creative and sensual energy.

- Luteal phase: This phase is associated with the Wild Woman or Goddess Kali, who represents transformation, renewal, and the release of old patterns. During this phase, women may choose to connect with Kali to gain insight, courage, and strength as they embark on a new cycle of growth and change.

You can choose to tap into your own biological rhythms if it feels good for you to do so and you might like to connect with the corresponding Goddess or season if you are drawn to them or their energy. For some Witches, this is the key to enhancing their practices and getting 'in flow'. Some even find they are synced to the Moon cycles too.

Whichever moon phase you bleed in (which does also change depending on what you are being called to focus your energies in to) holds its own power and magick for what you need to receive right now.

If you bleed during a dark to new moon, you're being called inwards to really connect with your wisdom and to nourish yourself, tend to your needs and enjoy your self care practices.

Should your period arrive during the waxing moon, you are being guided to discover something new. This is your time for exploration, growth and learning on a soul level.

For full moon menstruating babes, this is your time to shine. Get yourself out there and share you creations. (No coincidence my cycle has synced with the full moon in time for releasing this book!) This is time to be action woman!

If you have your bleed at the waning moon phase, you are refining and organising all the finer details right now. Your clarity is at its peak and you are able to develop new plans that really serve your intentions.

If any of this feels forced or your rhythms seem unpredictable or changeable, then don't worry, you don't have to utilise these cycles if they don't fit for you. Your life, your magick, your rules.

Womb Wisdom & Sexual Power

As a womb keeper and healer, I couldn't write a book and not mention just how sacred your womb space is. Whether you have a physical womb or not, whether you have a menstrual cycle or take contraception or hormones, this space is precious. It is also one of you sacred keys to manifestation as the portal of creation. Your deepest desires and passions, your inspiration and sexual power.

As part of our unfortunate history (*his – story*) of what happened to our ancestors and the witches before us, we have been very much conditioned to be ashamed of this part of us. Banished to red tents during our bleed; not permitted to be near men while we were 'hysterical'; encouraged by doctors to have a 'hysterectomy' to remedy our psychosis; convinced during orgasm that we invoked the devil; our pleasure was forbidden. Our connection to our womb, to our power, has been supressed, not to mention our most incredible tool to manifest – during climax! I had womb healing for myself to rid of the shame associated with being a woman, embarrassed from the age of 11 when I started my periods and waking up one morning to find I was a C cup before I reached high school. Ashamed and uncertain about sexual desires, who was deserving of my womb space, trauma and loss all stored away in this little pouch.

It is said that we carry all our ancestors trauma in our wombs too, even if we don't know who they are or where we came from, their experiences are all part of us (the divine oneness). This includes a generous helping of all of their baggage and generational wounds, all of which can lead us to a loss of creativity, power, confidence and medical manifestations like PCOS, infertility and menstruation hell. If you can find a womb healing circle in your area, this is your calling to go. It is part of my mission to pass on this healing to as many women as I can. Healing our wombs, our mothers, our ancestors and also healing Mother Earth. The womb is not a place to store fear and pain, it is a place to create and give birth to life.

As the portal to your manifesting and pleasure, it is always worth remembering the potency of your sexual energy. Our intimate pleasure is often a taboo subject and not as openly discussed as it can be for men. Perhaps the fear of a womans sexual power *is* justified, for it is during our moments of climax and orgasm that our vibration (no pun intended here) is at its peak for manifesting and attracting in extra juice (a little pun here) and joy in to our lives. I have known women who, very successfully I might add, have orgasmed over their desire (especially money) to manifest more of it. Sex magick is also being encouraged more and more in the witchy world too as a way of bringing partners closer together but also to manifest as a team effort! If ever you needed an excuse for more sexy time...you're welcome!

Magickal and Psychological Tools

We have already mentioned some key tools to utilise in your manifestation practices as you cross the 4D bridge, like gratitude, EFT and expanders, along with some wonderful magickal tools used in spells, such as crystals and other correspondences. The other tools in this chapter couldn't go unmentioned as they are hugely popular and/or some of my favourites. My clients have great success with these too and this is officially step seven of the manifestation process I teach.

Vision boards

This is creating a visual representation of your desired outcomes to help you to focus your thoughts and energy on manifesting your goals. This could be a physical board, like a collage, or a virtual board on Pinterest, or as your phone wallpaper.

Keep in mind that these boards will only work if you actually use them once you have created them. Don't get me wrong, the creative process is a beautiful manifestation ritual in its own right, especially if you set the scene and use a sacred space. But the power with vision boards comes from daily use so that you engage a part of your brain called your Reticular Activating System (RAS). This is a handy little built-in feature that supports you in finding ways of bringing you what you want. Why do we have post it notes with reminders stuck on our desk? So that our RAS will kick in and help us remember and complete those tasks.

Your brain will help you achieve your manifestations, you just have to keep it prominent as a frequent stimulus. This is exactly how posters and billboards work as marketing tools too.

If you are a visual learner who remembers information through looking at words and pictures, you will probably really like vision boards. You can select whatever images you feel represent your goals and even add on affirmations or motivational quotes and power words to inspire you. I have a peacock feather and key hanging on mine as well. You can include whatever you like! Be sure to have a photograph of you on your board (or a bitmoji) so that your RAS recognises that all your other images are connected to you too. A word of warning with your photograph: please do not use a photograph of you as a weight inspiration if you are trying to 'get back to what you were'. We cannot manifest backwards. You are co-creating a future and that means a future version of you. Ensure your photograph(s) truly represent you and who you are becoming.

When working with your board, you might like to meditate as you focus on each image and immerse yourself in the scene. Let it play out like a movie as a lovely little daydream. You could also write about each scene as a scripting exercise. Or you could visualise each scene from the viewpoint of an observer or someone else involved. For example, let's say you have a holiday on your vision board. You could write about a day on your holiday, from going to the airport, arriving at the hotel and hitting the beach with a cocktail, in a 'dear diary' kind of style. Alternatively, you could imagine all of these activities in your head and really feel the flip in your tummy as you take off, the warmth of the sunshine on your skin and the sand between your toes, and the utter relaxation as you settle into your hammock. Or perhaps you prefer to see it from your travel companion's perspective, as they take your photograph playing in the sea or stuffing your face at the all you can eat buffet. Or maybe even from the hotel staff's viewpoint, seeing you sunbathing as they try and encouraging you to join in aqua fit. Whatever visualisation angle you prefer, make note of how it makes you feel and prolong that feeling where you can. This shifts your vibration to the same frequency as your desire and that is one of the ways it can reach us quicker.

Anything on your board that makes you feel bad, like a failure or that it is out of reach, take it off. The same as having clothes that are too small in your wardrobe. If it is bringing down your vibe, it has no place in your space. Declutter.

Affirmations

We have mentioned these a few times already as they are so powerful. Positive affirmations are statements that help to shift your focus and energy towards your desired outcomes. You might hear these called mantras, which are repetitive phrases that can help to focus the mind and cultivate positive energy. Witches often use incantations too. These are exactly the same, sometimes rhyme, and we tend to sing or chant them. I personally prefer statements of intent that state what I will be doing/ having or becoming. You will probably find you have a preference and I find with my clients this links to their learning style and personality.

Reframing

Or rewiring of negative thoughts and beliefs into positive ones can help to improve your self-belief and support manifestation. You may have already noticed some patterns in your negative thoughts, or certain situations or people that make your vibe dip. Once you have identified these or caught yourself in the moment of your negative thought or feeling, you can work on reframing and rewiring.

I think this process can sometimes feel overly simplistic, and it is not to say that it is difficult to do; it really is a simple as it seems in terms of the process. However, keep in mind that it does take time and repetition. Some of your beliefs may stem from your childhood or even from your ancestors. It could be decades or centuries worth of baggage and BS (belief system or, you know, bullshit) that your brain has become super familiar with and is so ingrained in your subconscious. Go easy on yourself if it takes a little while to shift.

One of my favourite ways is to think about the polar opposite of the negative thought. For example, believing *"This is the worst time to set up a business during an economic crisis/ global pandemic/ other bonkers world event"* is enough to put any aspiring entrepreneur down in the dumps. The opposite of this would be to think that *"This is the best time to set up a business as there is so much uncertainty and instability in my employment and other people need my help more than ever right now."* It may feel unbelievable in the moment, and I empathise because this was one of my own negative thoughts that was on repeat when I set up my coaching business at the start of the Covid19 pandemic in 2020.

The next stage really helps - we get to play detective. I would like you to compile evidence for both of these statements to bring to my courtroom of magick and enchantment. How much evidence to you have for each? Is it a fact that this is the worst time for you? Is this true for every other entrepreneur on the planet? Is nobody starting up a business right now? Or were top companies like Disney, Netflix and Uber actually set up during similar economic crises? If your negative statement isn't true for every other human being, 100% of the time, then you will be dismissed from my courtroom for telling porkies to the jury!

Your next step is to do a cost-benefits analysis. Let's take another example. Perhaps each day after work you feel like *"I am a really bad sales consultant."* Flip this to *"I am the best sales consultant in the company."*

It might feel far-fetched, but which one will ultimately serve you better? How much is it costing you to believe in the negative? Financially, emotionally, physically and personally it has an impact. What would the benefits be of believing in the positive? Remember our natural avoidance of pain and gravitation towards pleasure.

There are so many other ways of working on your limiting beliefs, your mindset and reframing your psyche. This is what us coaches are for, and we all have our own methods and toolbox. You will find tons of additional supportive resources online too.

Remember, it may feel overly simple to just focus on the opposite of your feeling, but with consistency it does truly begin to alter your mindset. Dig as deep as you can with this, work with a coach to do some shadow mapping and keep checking in on that fight or flight response too.

Scripting

Scripting involves writing down your desired outcome as if it has already happened. This helps to clarify your goals, activate your subconscious mind, and bring your dreams into your reality. I like to do this as a 'Dear Diary' style exercise, along with utilising my vision board, or taking it one step further and creating written materials that support my desires. E.g, a resignation letter, or job offer.

Dreamwork

If you are somebody who doesn't get into a deep enough REM sleep to dream, this one may be a challenge as it involves paying close attention to your dreams. It involves interpreting symbols, colours, scenes, characters and using as much information from your dreams to support your manifestation. This can be done through journaling, meditation, or working with a dream analyst or mentor.

I encourage my clients to record their dreams in as much detail upon waking as they can, even if it is just doodles or a voice note summary. Include the time and date and you can start to observe patterns between your dreams and your waking life. Your dreams are your subconscious messages that want to be heard. It may be that you are manifesting a new home and you dream about a certain part of the country you have never been to before. This could be a signal that you need to look in a different area. Perhaps you are having trouble with your work colleagues, and you have a dream about your boss being sick. Maybe this is a reminder that we are all human, we are all connected, and could you potentially help bring the team together if your boss is unable to do so?

You could also supplement your dream work with a lovely method I have used since I was a child – the pillow method. This involves placing affirmations, questions, or objects under your pillow while you sleep to enhance your dream recall and messages. This is believed to help reprogram your subconscious mind and align your thoughts with what is under your pillow. I did this with all of my revision notes from GCSE's right through to my master's to help me remember everything and I never got lower than a B grade in any exam (nerd alert!)

555

The 555 method is a manifestation technique where you write down your desired outcome five times a day for five days. This helps to reinforce your goals and focus your energy on them in a similar way to affirmations. Ideal for any fellow writers out there, although this sometimes feels like you are in detention and writing lines. I recommend nice gel pens in your corresponding magickal colour to help give this a boost. There are also the 365 and 777 methods which are similar practices. Perhaps create your own and use the numbers that also correspond to your intention!

Placebos:

Not just for the medical and pharmaceutical world, placebos are objects or actions that are believed to bring about a desired outcome, even if they have no scientific basis for doing so. In the context of manifestation, a placebo can be used to symbolise your desired outcome. For example, if you take vitamins every day and you are trying to manifest more self-confidence, you could label your vitamin box *"confidence tablets"*. Or if you are attracting in more wealth, you could personalise your water bottle as *"wealth juice"*.

Sounds silly, but it is simple and effective as well as being a bit of fun.

Energy work

Practices like meditation, Reiki, or chakra balancing can help to align your energy with your desired outcome, as well as with the identity of the superhero you are becoming. Similarly, energy mapping, where you map out your goals, desired outcomes, and action steps in a visual format, can help to clarify your intentions and track your progress alongside your energy healing practice.

Check out your local community for Reiki practitioners, sound baths, womb healing circles, shamanic drumming journeys or cacao ceremonies. Once you start looking, you will be surprised at how many options for energy healing work that you find (manifest). A lot of practitioners, me included, have been running these online since the pandemic too. So don't worry if you are in a rural area or somewhere where there are little in person opportunities, the internet is full of supportive lightworkers who can help you with this.

Focus Wheels

A focus wheel is a visual representation of your goals and desired outcomes. It consists of a central circle with spokes radiating out from the centre to create sections. Each section represents a specific aspect of your desired outcome. For example, if you have a body or health goal, your sections may have results such as 'dream wedding dress', 'confident in a bikini on holiday', 'happier to have sex with the lights on' etc. By focusing on each section and visualising the outcome, you align your vibration, just the same as with a vision board.

This is a nice alternative to a vision board as it can be used for each individual goal or desire that you have. You can also alter it slightly so that each section is an action step, if you would rather use this as a daily reminder of what to do in order to align with your intentions. E.g, Walk 1 mile, drink 3 litres of water, have fruit for breakfast etc. I also like that it looks like a lemon!

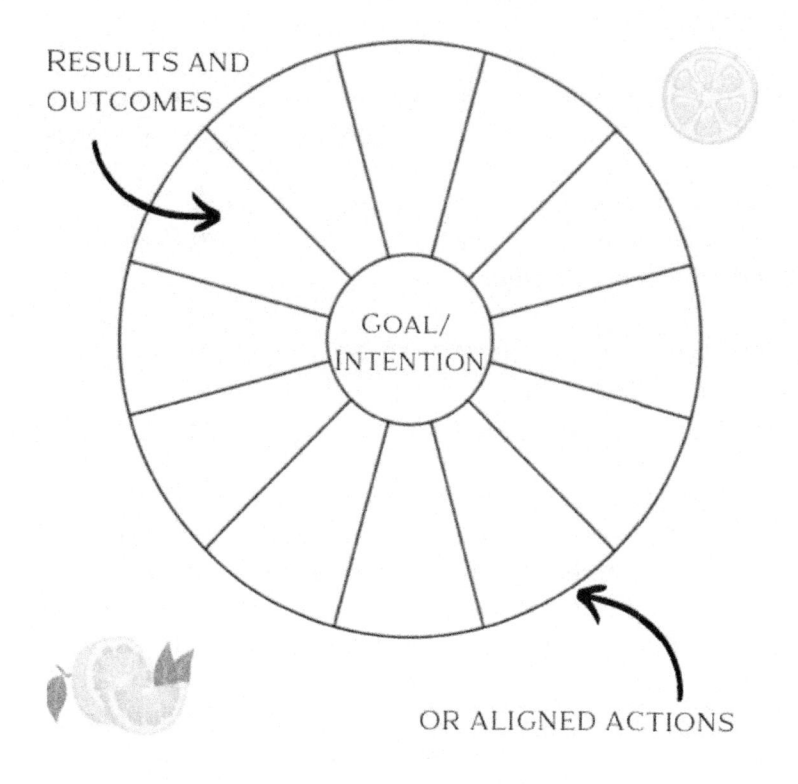

RESULTS AND OUTCOMES

GOAL/ INTENTION

OR ALIGNED ACTIONS

Two Cups Method

Surprise- this involves two cups! One to represent what you want to manifest and one to represent what you're releasing. You label the cup representing what you want to manifest with symbols, images, or words that represent your desired outcome. The cup representing what you're releasing is labelled with symbols, images, or words that represent negative thoughts, limiting beliefs, or habits that are holding you back.

You then fill the releasing cup with water (or wine, no judgement) and feel all those elements holding you back and remembering why you want to let them go. As you pour the liquid manifestation super juice from your release cup into the manifesting cup, imagine all of those setbacks and limitations flowing away.

Finally, drink from your manifesting cup and absorb all the new goodies that you are calling in and physically digesting into your body and being. Cheers!

It's important to experiment with different techniques and find what works best for you. You will probably enjoy different methods for different goals and find some that don't feel right for you, as well as others that are your fail-safe methods. What's most important above everything else, is that you have that clear intention and take consistent action towards your goals. Remember that manifestation is a holistic process that involves the mind, body, and spirit. Combining psychological and magickal tools along with physical actions and rituals can help to create a more powerful manifestation experience. The witch way.

Spells & Manifestation Boosters

Witchcraft can be a powerful tool for boosting your life in whatever way you desire. I am hoping that you are beginning to see this now and that you may have been practicing witchcraft already. By using the principles of manifestation, energy work, and intention-setting, you can harness the power of magick to attract success, abundance, and opportunities to your personal and professional life.

Career and Business

Here are some ways to use witchcraft to boost your career or business:

- Set clear intentions: One of the most important aspects of witchcraft is setting clear intentions. Take some time to clarify your intentions and visualise what you really want to achieve in your career or business. I often see misalignment between what we think we want and what we actually want on a soul level that is based on our values. This happens most frequently when it come to our professional lives and trying to battle with our ego and making others proud rather than being concerned with our true desires and life purpose. Write down your goals and intentions, check for any negative consequences and other potential subconscious sabotages (have someone help you if needs be) and then keep your goals in a place where you can see them regularly and check in on your progress. Go back to the chapter on intentions for a refresh.

- Create a ritual: To help you to focus your energy and intentions on your career or business goals. Choose a time and place where you can be uninterrupted and create a sacred space that feels comfortable and inspiring. Light candles, burn incense, or use other tools that help you to connect with your intuition and the magick of the universe. You can use some of the tools we have mentioned in this book- perhaps a business focused vision board or write your dream job description whilst you are in your sacred space and the vibration is high. See yourself receiving a promotion, signing a new contract, or attracting new clients. Feel the emotions of success and abundance, and let these feelings infuse your energy and actions.

- Work with the elements: The elements of earth, air, fire, and water are important in witchcraft, and can be used to boost your career or business. For example, earth can help you to ground your energy and focus on practical matters, while fire can help you to be more assertive and confident. Water can help you to flow with the energy of the universe, while air can help you to communicate more effectively and make new connections. If you have a business plan to write, get outside if you can or surround yourself with crystals or plants for that earth element. Got a job interview coming up? Get yourself around a fire pit the night before and burn any concerns you have on little pieces of paper. Even write a resignation letter to your current boss and burn it in preparation. There is no clearer signal to the universe that you are ready!

Business Boss Babe

New Moon

Tuesday, Thursday or Saturday

Materials

A yellow candle

A piece of aventurine or citrine crystal

A piece of paper and a pen

A fireproof dish or bowl

Essential Oil (optional)

Instructions

Set up your altar and sacred space, cast your circle and call on your supporters (I would go for the Horned God for some stability and discipline).

Anoint the candle or yourself with your choice of oil if you wish, and light the candle.

Take a few deep breaths, hold your crystal, and ground yourself in the present moment. Allow yourself to feel calm and centered. Play chilled music or sound frequencies if you like.

On the piece of paper, write down your intention to start a successful business. Be specific about what you want to achieve and how you plan to do it. Visualise your business thriving and growing, as well as what this means for you and others.

Hold the crystal in your other hand and meditate on its energy. Aventurine and Citrine are both known for their abundance and prosperity energies, making them excellent for business success spells.

Imagine the crystal radiating a warm, golden light that fills your body and mind with positive energy.
With the crystal still in your hand, recite the following incantation:

"By the power of Earth and Sun, I call forth the energy of abundance and prosperity. May this crystal be a magnet for success, drawing in new opportunities and good fortune. As I start this new business venture, may it be infused with positive energy and prosperity. So mote it be."

Light the piece of paper on fire using the candle flame and place it in the fireproof dish or bowl. As you watch the paper burn, see any doubts or fears about starting a business being released and transformed into positive energy.

Take the crystal and hold it up to the candle flame, allowing the light to pass through it. This is believed to amplify the crystal's energy and intention. (Be careful not to burn your fingers) See the crystal radiating its energy out into the universe and bringing in the energy of success and prosperity.

Allow the candle to burn down completely (use tea lights if you like).

Carry the crystal with you or place it on your desk as a reminder of your intention and to help draw in success and abundance. Close your circle, thank your guides and supporters and wash your hands.

You Better Work Witch

Waxing Moon

Tuesday, Wednesday or Sunday

Materials

An orange candle

A piece of paper and a pen

A fireproof dish or bowl

A few drops of essential oil (optional)

Instructions

Set up your altar and sacred space, cast your circle and call on your supporters (I like Freya for work related spells).

Anoint the candle or yourself with your choice of oil if you wish, and light the candle.

Take a few deep breaths and ground yourself in the present moment. Allow yourself to feel calm and centered. Play chilled music or sound frequencies if you like.

On the piece of paper, write down the qualities you desire in a new job. Be as specific as possible, including details about the type of work, salary, location, and company culture.

Hold the paper in your hands and visualise yourself in your ideal job. See yourself working in a fulfilling career that brings you joy and satisfaction. Feel the positive energy of this visualisation flowing through your body.

If you have a specific company or job in mind, take a few moments to see yourself getting the job offer. Imagine yourself receiving a phone call or email with the good news. (You could even write the job offer or contract to work with daily or pin on your vision board).

Light the piece of paper on fire using the candle flame and place it in the fireproof dish or bowl. As you watch the paper burn, say the following words:

"By the power of the flame, I release my desire into the universe. I attract a new job that brings me joy, fulfilment, and financial abundance. As I watch this paper burn, my intention is released and the universe hears my call. So mote it be."

Allow the candle to burn down completely (use a tea light if you like).

Take any remaining ashes from the burned paper and scatter them outside. As you do so, see your desire for a new job being released into the universe and taking root.

Close your circle, thank your guides and supporters and wash your hands.

Abundance

Using witchcraft to boost your money can involve a variety of practices and techniques. Here are a few examples:

- Visualisation: Seeing yourself as having financial abundance is a powerful way to manifest money as it takes your focus away from the physical cash (which is just a currency that is intended to flow in and out) and towards what you actually want the money for. Try visualising yourself having the money you need, how you are using it and feeling grateful for it.

- Work with abundance-enhancing crystals: There are several crystals that are known for their ability to attract abundance and prosperity, such as Citrine, Pyrite, and Green Aventurine. You can carry these crystals with you, wear them as jewellery, or place them in your workspace or around your money plants to enhance their energy.

- Money altar: Creating a money altar can be an effective way to focus your intentions and energy on wealth and abundance. Decorate it with items that represent prosperity, such as green candles, money-drawing herbs or plants, luxury items, pictures of wealth (or Goddess Lakshmi) and of course, cash! Spend time each day connecting with the energy of your altar and focusing your intention on attracting more abundance. Being surrounded by wealth anchors and reminders allows you to energetically align but also to feel safe in the presence of abundance so that it flows to you with ease.

Money Does Grow On Trees

Waxing Moon

Thursday

Materials

A healthy and thriving plant (ideally one that is associated with abundance, such as a jade plant or money tree)

A green candle

A piece of paper and a pen

Any crystals or other items associated with abundance (optional)

Instructions

Set up your sacred space, cast your circle and call on your supporters. (Lakshmi is my go to Goddess for abundance).

Take a few deep breaths to ground yourself and focus your energy. Light the green candle and take a few moments to gaze at the flame, focusing your intention on attracting abundance and wealth.

On the piece of paper, write down any financial goals or desires that you have. Be as specific and detailed as possible, and try to focus on what you want to manifest, rather than what you want to avoid.

Hold the piece of paper in your hands and visualise your financial goals coming to fruition. Imagine what it would feel like to have abundance and financial security in your life.

Place the piece of paper under the pot or soil of the plant. As you do so, say the following incantation or one that resonates with you:

"Money grows and wealth abounds, In my life it knows no bounds. I call upon this plant to bring abundance, wealth, and everything. So mote it be."

If you have any crystals or other items associated with abundance, you can place them near the plant to amplify the energy of the spell.

Take a few moments to meditate and focus on your breath, allowing yourself to be open and receptive to abundance and wealth.

When you feel ready, blow out or snuff the candle and thank the plant for its help in attracting abundance into your life. Close your circle, thank your guides and wash your hands.

Self-Love

Self-love is a fundamental aspect of our well-being, and witchcraft can be a powerful tool to help us cultivate self-love and acceptance. Here are some ways you can use witchcraft to boost your self-love:

- Create affirmations: Be sure your affirmations resonate with you, such as *"I am worthy of love and respect,"* and repeat them to yourself regularly. Pop them on a post it note or write it on your mirror in lippy. Keep them where you will see them as a prompt to say them, preferably while admiring your own reflection. You could also add photos of self-love Goddesses such as Aphrodite, Freya, and Hathor and have an army of beauty queens on your dressing table.

- Practice self-care: Self-care is an essential aspect of self-love as it is the practical side to loving our physical vessel. Take time to do things that make you feel good, such as taking a bath, meditating, or spending time in nature. You can also create a self-care altar or ritual that helps you connect with your own needs and desires. I suggest my clients use a pleasure menu that has a list of quick and easy self-care 'pick me ups' that they can go to at the drop of a hat.

- Set boundaries: Or as I like to refer to them: standards. This is an important aspect of self-love. By setting clear boundaries with others and standards with yourself, you send a message to the universe that you are honouring your own needs and desires, which cultivates a sense of self-worth so your manifestations flow.

It may feel alien if you are used to being a people pleaser (which is actually a form of victimising yourself and not a 'good person trait' to have at all – that's for another book!). However, for the most part, others will have more respect for you. If they don't, they are a bunch of tossers who don't deserve you. Keep in mind that standards don't make you an asshole, they are there to protect you and others, and so that you can be a better girlfriend, husband, friend or sibling.

Beauty Queen Glow Getter

New or Waxing Moon

Tuesday, Thursday, Friday or Sunday

Materials
Carrier oil (such as sweet almond oil, jojoba oil, or coconut oil)
Essential oils (such as lavender, rose, geranium, or frankincense)
A small glass bottle with a dropper or pump top
A crystal of your choice

Instructions

Set up your sacred space, cast your circle and call on your supporters (I would go for the Aphrodite). You can also light candles and incense for a boost with this spell. Create your magick space how you wish.

In the small glass bottle, pour in the carrier oil of your choice, leaving a bit of space at the top for the essential oils and crystal.

Choose your essential oils, keeping in mind their magical correspondences. For example, lavender is associated with beauty and relaxation, rose with love and self-love, geranium with confidence, and frankincense with spirituality and healing. Add a few drops of each oil to the carrier oil, making sure to blend well.

Hold the crystal in your hands and visualise its energy infusing the oil with beauty, confidence, and self-love. You may wish to chant a mantra or incantation to help focus your intention.

Add the crystal to the oil mixture, then seal the bottle and shake it gently to blend the ingredients.

When you are ready to use the beauty oil, shake the bottle to mix the ingredients, then apply a small amount to your skin, focusing on areas where you want to feel beautiful and confident. Take a moment to breathe in the scent of the oils and to feel their energy uplifting and supporting you.

As you apply the oil, repeat positive affirmations to yourself, such as "*I am beautiful and confident*" or "*I radiate love and self-love.*" Allow yourself to feel gorgeous and confident, knowing that you have created this magickal moisturiser to support you in your journey.

I would probably play some boss babe empowering songs at the same time and belt out some tunes!

Close your circle, thank your guides and wash your hands.

Goddess Love Bath

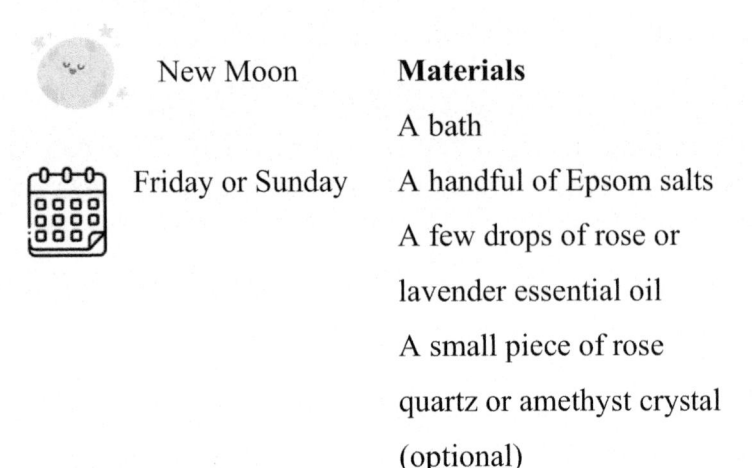

New Moon

Friday or Sunday

Materials

A bath

A handful of Epsom salts

A few drops of rose or lavender essential oil

A small piece of rose quartz or amethyst crystal (optional)

Instructions

Set up your sacred bathroom space and call on your supporters (I would go for the Aphrodite on this one). You can also light candles and incense for a boost with this spell. Create your bathing sanctuary how you wish.

As the water is running, add a handful of Epsom salts or sea salt to the water. Salt is believed to purify and cleanse the energy field and can help release any negative emotions or self-doubt.

Add a few drops of rose or lavender essential oil to the water. Rose is associated with love and self-love, while lavender is known for its calming and soothing properties. Both are excellent for promoting self-love and self-care, but you are free to select oils that you like and feel drawn to use.

If desired, you can place a small piece of rose quartz or amethyst crystal in the water (if they aren't soluble!) or by the bath. These crystals are associated with the heart chakra and can help open and heal the heart center, promoting self-love and compassion.

As you soak in the water visualise any negative self-talk or self-doubt being washed away. See the water carrying away any negative energy and leaving you feeling refreshed and renewed.

Take deep breaths and focus on sending love and compassion to yourself. Repeat positive affirmations to yourself, such as "*I am worthy of love and happiness*" or "*I am enough just as I am.*" (You could even write these in the steam of the bathroom mirror).

When you feel ready, slowly get out of the bath. Take a moment to feel grateful for the opportunity to take care of yourself and to focus on self-love.

Carry the crystals with you as a self-love 'anchor'.

Close your circle, thank your guides and supporters and follow up with a good moisturising massage sesh - especially for your feet and ankles to ground yourself.

Remember to be kind and compassionate with yourself, and trust in the power of magick to help you cultivate more self-love and acceptance. You are capable of creating a deeper connection with yourself that promotes a sense of respect and wellbeing that will truly benefit every aspect of your life.

Health

As the natural healers of the world and the leading lads and lasses of plant medicine, witches know the most powerful tools to help boost your health and wellness. By working with the elements, natural world, and energies around us, you can harness the power of magick to promote healing and well-being. This is not a substitute for seeking medical advice if your leg is about to fall off!

Here are some ways you can use witchcraft to boost your health and wellness:

- Use herbal remedies: Herbs have been used for centuries for their healing properties. You can create herbal remedies, such as teas or tinctures, to support your physical health. Research which herbs are best for your specific needs and consult with a qualified herbalist or healthcare professional before using them. You can also add certain herbs to your cooking or make yourself a 'bath bag' (like a tea bag but for your bath!)

- Perform healing spells and rituals: Healing spells can be a powerful way to promote healing and are usually nice and quick. You can create your own spell using candles, crystals, and herbs, or find one that resonates with you online, or in a woo woo spell book. The key is to focus your energy and intention on your health goals and trust in the power of magick to support your healing journey. That intention is key!

- Gratitude: Practicing gratitude for your body and its abilities is a powerful way to attract health and wellness. Remember the gratitude rock story? Try writing down things you are grateful for each day, focusing on the good health you already have, and the extra dose of wellness that the universe is sending you.

If your health and mental wellbeing is a priority for you then I can't recommend working with a coach or other health professional enough. I may be biased as a holistic wellbeing coach myself, but these wizards of wellness have helped me overcome anxiety and depression when nothing else was working… don't be afraid to ask for help, your health is the most important thing you have!

The Well Witches Brew

Any

Any

Materials

A teapot or infuser

A selection of healing herbs and spices (such as chamomile, peppermint, ginger, turmeric, cinnamon, or nettle)

A kettle of hot water

A cup or mug

Honey or other sweetener (optional)

Instructions

Set up your sacred kitchen space and call on your supporters (I call on the Goddess each morning for this one).

In the teapot or infuser, place a selection of healing herbs and spices, keeping in mind their magickal correspondences. For example, chamomile is associated with relaxation and restful sleep; peppermint with digestion and focus; ginger with immune support; turmeric with anti-inflammatory properties; cinnamon with warmth and comfort; and nettle with overall wellness. Mix and match the herbs and spices to suit your needs and taste.

Bring a kettle of water to a boil, then pour the hot water over the herbs and spices in the teapot or infuser. Allow the tea to steep for a few minutes, until it reaches the desired strength and flavour.

While the tea is steeping, take a few moments to visualise the healing energy of the herbs and spices infusing the water with health and wellbeing. You may wish to chant a mantra or incantation to help focus your intention.

When the tea is ready, strain it into a cup or mug, adding honey or another sweetener if desired. Take a moment to breathe in the aroma of the tea and to feel its warmth and energy nourishing your body and soul.

As you drink the tea, focus on the healing properties of the herbs and spices, allowing them to support your health and wellbeing. Repeat positive affirmations to yourself, such as "*I am healthy and well*" or "*My body is strong and vibrant.*"

Allow yourself to feel the healing energy of the tea, knowing that you have created this magickal elixir to support you in your journey. And of course – see what messages you can see in your tea leaves!

Mirror Mirror On The Wall

Full or Waning Moon

Any

Materials

A small handheld mirror

A white or yellow candle

A piece of paper and a pen

Any herbs or crystals associated with health and positivity (optional)

Instructions

Set up your sacred space, cast your circle and call on your supporters. I usually ask my angels to help bring in good health and wellbeing, or Goddess Kali for a fresh slate.

Hold the mirror in your hands, and gaze into it for a few moments. Visualise a radiant and healthy version of yourself reflected back at you.

Write down on the piece of paper any health concerns or issues that you want to release or improve. It could be a physical ailment, a bad habit, or any other obstacles that are impacting your well-being.

Hold the paper in your hands and read your list out loud. As you do so, feel yourself letting go of these negative energies and any blockages that are preventing you from being in good health.

Take a few moments to meditate and focus on your breath, allowing yourself to be open and receptive to positive energy and healing.

If you have any herbs or crystals associated with health and positivity, you can sprinkle them around the candle or hold them in your hands to amplify the energy of the spell.

Hold the mirror up to the candle flame, allowing the light to reflect off of it. Imagine this light filling your body and bringing healing and positive energy to every part of your being.

When you feel ready, blow out the candle and place the mirror in a safe and secure location where it won't be disturbed. Close your circle, thank your guides and wash your hands.

Remember to trust in your power to support your healing journey and be open to new possibilities and opportunities for wellness. Achieving your weight and health goals is not just about spells and rituals, but also about making healthy choices and taking action towards your goals too. Show the universe that you love and respect your body and that you fully intend to care and nurture yourself.

Love

Witchcraft can be a powerful tool to help boost your love and sex life as you can harness the power of magick to enhance intimacy and connection with your partner. This is not to be used to manipulate another person or get them to do something against their will. The rule of 3 and 'harm none' always applies.

Here are some ways you can use witchcraft to (safely) boost your love and sex life:

- Create a love boudoir: Creating a dedicated space in your bedroom (or dedicating the entire room) for love magick can help to focus your energy as you live and breathe love, passion and romance. Add items to your sex den, sorry, bedroom, that represent love and passion to you. This might be candles, pictures, oils, sex toys, luxurious bedding and cushions, a new silk robe and lingerie. Whatever brings you the vibe (ahem) that you desire.

- Use love and passion-enhancing herbs and fragrances: Herbs and oils have been used for centuries in seduction. You can create herbal remedies, such as love potions, to support your romantic and sexual desires, or oils and fragrances, for cultivating passion and sexual confidence.

- Practice intimacy and connection-building activities: These can help to deepen your relationship with your partner and enhance your sex life. Try activities such as couples' yoga, sensual massage, rose ceremonies or tantric practices to build trust and connection with your partner.

- Divination: Tarot and oracle readings are most often utilised for help with love and romance. They can provide insight into your love life and help you identify any blocks that may be hindering your progress. Consult a reader or mystic or create a love spread with your own cards to focus specifically on matters of the heart. If you are a beginner with oracle or tarot cards then try choosing 3 cards at random, the first to represent your recent past when it comes to love, the second to indicate your current energy and situation, and the third to guide you on your next best steps and where to focus your energy. Always make a note of your cards with the date of your reading, use your intuition to help you interpret them, being sure to check for symbols and correspondences in the artwork, and come back to your notes when you feel the need.

Love Me Pillow Pouch

New or Waxing Moon

Friday

Materials

A small pouch or sachet (preferably red or pink)

A small piece of rose quartz

Dried lavender or rose petals

A needle and thread (preferably red)

A small piece of paper and a pen

Optional: any other love-related items such as herbs, crystals, or charms

Instructions

Set up your sacred space, cast your circle and call on your supporters. (I would say Venus for lasting love, Aphrodite for a more saucy relationship, or both for a double whammy).

Take the small piece of paper and write down the qualities and attributes that you desire in a romantic partner. Be as specific as possible, and focus on the positive qualities you wish to attract. I would especially focus on the feelings and how you want this relationship to be.

Fold the piece of paper and place it in the pouch, along with the dried lavender or rose petals and the piece of rose quartz. If you have any other love-related items, you can add them as well.

Sew the pouch shut with the red thread, while focusing your intention on attracting love and romance into your life. You can say an incantation or simply focus on your desire for love and connection.

Once the pouch is securely closed, hold it in your hands and visualise yourself surrounded by love and happiness. Imagine yourself meeting the perfect romantic partner, and feel the joy and excitement that comes with being in a loving relationship.

Once you feel the energy of the pouch, place it inside a small pillow or cushion. You can use any colour or style that you like, but try to choose one that feels romantic or cosy.

Place the pillow on your bed or in another area of your home where you spend a lot of time. You can also carry the pouch with you in your pocket or purse.

Close your circle, thank your guides and wash your hands. When you want to activate the energy of the pouch, hold it in your hands and see yourself surrounded by love and happiness. You can also say a quick affirmation or incantation, such as "*Love surrounds me always*" or "*I am open to the love that is coming to me.*"

Save The Date

New or Waxing Moon

Tuesday, Friday or Sunday

Materials

A small piece of rose quartz, aventurine or tigers eye

A sprig of rosemary

A white and red candle

A piece of paper and a pen

Instructions

Set up your sacred space, cast your circle and call on your supporters (I would go for Venus or Aphrodite for all love spells).

Light the candles and sit quietly in front of them, taking a few deep breaths to ground and centre yourself. Play relaxing or romantic music if you wish.

Take the crystal(s) and hold in your left hand. Close your eyes and visualise a warm, pink light emanating from the crystal(s) and enveloping your body. Imagine this light filling you with confidence, self-love, and positive energy about your date.

Next, take the sprig of rosemary and hold it in your right hand. Imagine a bright, cleansing energy radiating from the herb and enveloping your aura. Imagine this energy clearing away any doubts, fears, or negative thoughts that may be holding you back.

With the pen and paper, write down some affirmations that make you feel confident and powerful. For example, "*I am worthy of love and respect*", "*I am beautiful and deserving of happiness*", or "*I trust in my own intuition and strength*". Use whatever affirmations resonate with you personally. Read your affirmations out loud, seeing each one coming true in your life. Feel the confidence and self-love growing within you as you speak.

When you feel ready, blow or snuff out the candles and carry the crystal(s) and rosemary with you on your date. You can keep them in your pocket, purse, or anywhere else that feels comfortable and convenient.

Throughout your date, whenever you feel your confidence faltering or your nerves getting the best of you, take a moment to hold the crystal(s) and/or the rosemary and cultivate the positive energy and affirmations you invoked in the spell.

Remember that the most important thing is to be yourself and enjoy the experience. This spell is simply a tool to help you tap into your own inner strength and beauty, and to remind yourself of the love and worthiness that already reside within you.

Close your circle, thank your guides and wash your hands. Now go and smash your date! (Not literally.... unless it goes very well....!)

Friendship

As a nomadic witch who has relocated and travelled solo around the world, I know the importance of attracting your tribe and the benefits of a strong sisterhood. Witchcraft can be used to help you strengthen and deepen your friendship circle as well as finding your soul mates and kindred spirits. You can also use magick to promote a sense of community and connection.

Here are some ways you can use witchcraft to boost your friendship circle:

- Work with friendship-enhancing herbs: There are several herbs that are known for their ability to enhance friendship and promote a sense of community, such as lavender, chamomile, and rose. You can create herbal remedies, such as teas, and incorporate them into your daily routine, or perhaps bake with them and have a tea party for your new friends.

- Use divination tools: Such as oracle cards or pendulums to help you gain insight into your friendships and understand how to strengthen them. Spend time each day connecting with your intuition, your angels and guides, and using your divination tools to guide your actions. This can be especially helpful if you have some friends that have become distant, and you aren't sure why or if there is something you can do to help.

- Connect with the energy of community: Spend time in your community and promoting a sense of connection with others. You can attend events in your local area, volunteer, or join online groups that share your interests. This will help you attract like-minded individuals who can become lifelong friends. Ask any of my Goddesses who have been on any of my retreats – they are sisters for life!

Attract Your Tribe

New or Waxing Moon

Wednesday, Thursday or Sunday

Materials

A small piece of paper and a pen

A pink candle

A small bowl of water

A sprig of fresh mint

Instructions

Set up your sacred space, cast your circle and call on your supporters (I would go for Freya to hunt out new likeminded soul friends).

Light the pink candle and place it in front of you. Take the sprig of mint and hold it in your hands, visualising a bright, green energy radiating from the herb.

On the piece of paper, write down some qualities you would like your new friends to have. For example, "kind", "funny", "supportive", "adventurous", "creative", etc.

Hold the paper in your hands and read your list out loud. Imagine that you are sending out a message to the universe, calling in the energies of these qualities and inviting them into your life.

Next, dip the sprig of mint into the bowl of water and sprinkle a few drops onto the paper. Mint is associated with the energy of attraction and is said to draw positive energies towards you.

Take the paper and fold it into a small square. Hold it over the flame of the pink candle (carefully), allowing the fire to purify and infuse the paper with your intentions.

Once the paper has been charged, hold it over the bowl of water and sprinkle a few more drops of mint water onto it. As you do so, say the following incantation:

"New friends, come to me. With hearts open and spirits free. May our bond be strong and true. And bring joy to me and you"

Allow the candle to burn down completely (use a tea light if you like). When it is safe to do so, dispose of the candle and the paper outside, or in a fire-safe container.

Remember to keep an open mind and heart as you go about your day-to-day life. The friends you seek may come to you in unexpected ways, so be receptive to new opportunities and connections. Trust that the universe is working in your favour and that the energies you have invoked in this spell are already at work in your life.

Close your circle, thank your guides and wash your hands.

Banishing

Witchcraft can be used to banish negativity and promote a more positive, harmonious energy in your life. You can use magick to release negative energy and protect yourself from its influence, but remember, even with banishing magick, we must harm nobody or use it for manipulation. It will come back and bite you on the bum! But if someone is being a pest, I happily pop them in the freezer for a while…

Here are some ways you can use witchcraft to banish negativity and keep yourself safe:

- Work with protection-enhancing crystals: There are several crystals that are known for their ability to protect against negative energy, such as black tourmaline, amethyst, and hematite. You can carry these crystals with you, wear them as jewellery, or place them in or around your home as a protective shield. I always advise my baby witches to wear crystals such as these for protection when starting their spiritual practices or when encountering difficult situations that may be draining or if they need a few boundaries in place.

- Create a protective talisman: On a similar note, you can create a talisman, such as a mojo bag or amulet, to carry with you and protect against negative energy. Choose items that resonate with you, such as herbs, crystals, or symbols of protection. There are some beautiful Native American items widely available or creations from indigenous tribes that you may like to browse to find your protector. Alternatively, craft your own, especially if it includes a representation of your spirit animal or guide. Angel wings and dream catchers are a popular choice too.

- Practice mindfulness and self-care: These can be a simple yet powerful practices to help you release negative energy and promote a more positive, harmonious energy in your life. Spend time each day connecting with your inner self and taking care of your physical, emotional, and spiritual needs to keep that vibe in neutral or above.

Freeze MF!

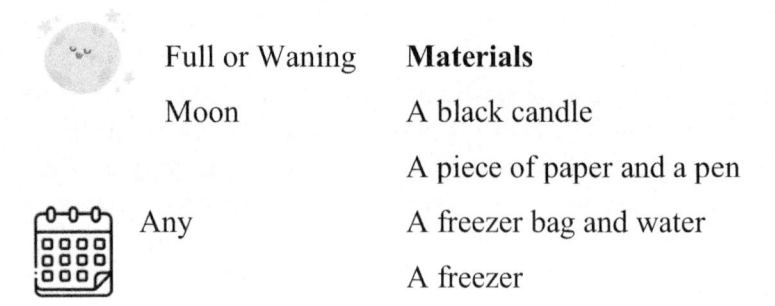

Full or Waning Moon

Any

Materials

A black candle

A piece of paper and a pen

A freezer bag and water

A freezer

Instructions

Set up your sacred space, cast your circle and call on your supporters (I would go for Hecate on this one but be wary, she takes no prisoners). Only use this spell to freeze someone or a situation if you are absolutely sure you want it gone from your life. You mustn't use this to harm anybody and remember the rule of 3- your intentions will come back threefold. I would only use this when I need someone to back off and give me some space. I will take them out of the freezer if and when I am ready.

Light your candle and write down the name of the person or details of the situation you want to take a break from.

Fold the paper away from you and place it in your freezer bag with some water. You can also add in some protective herbs if you like, you are keeping the frozen person safe, just away from you!

Pop it in the freezer and visualise all parties involved feeling 'cooled off' and happier about the situation at hand.

Allow the candle to burn down completely. Close your circle, thank your guides and wash your hands.

You can reverse this spell simply by taking the bag out of the freezer and allowing it to defrost but keep in mind they may be frozen and banished for good if that is how it is meant to be.

Your Home Your Sanctuary

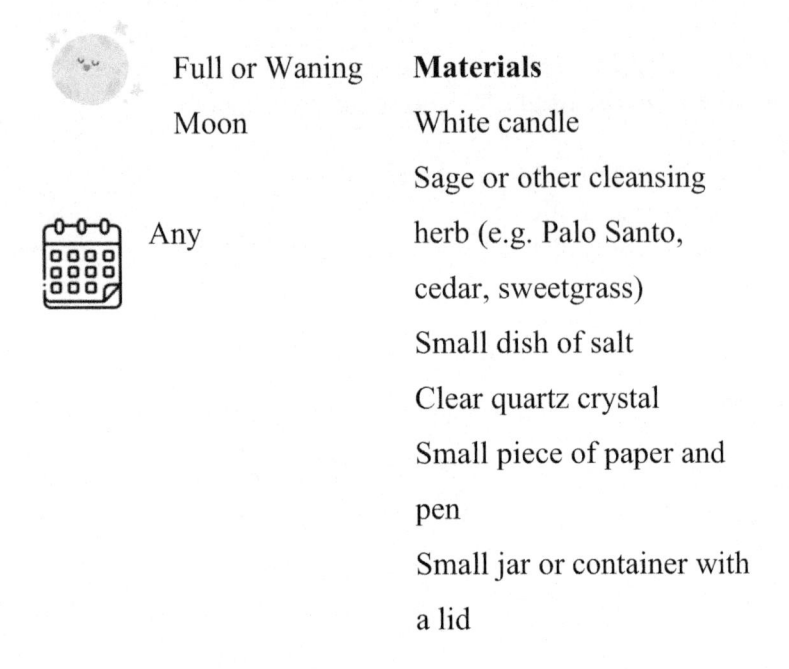

Full or Waning Moon

Any

Materials

White candle

Sage or other cleansing herb (e.g. Palo Santo, cedar, sweetgrass)

Small dish of salt

Clear quartz crystal

Small piece of paper and pen

Small jar or container with a lid

Instructions

Set up your sacred space, cast your circle and call on your supporters (I would go for Brigid for all home spells).

Begin by cleansing your home with sage or another cleansing herb. Light the herb and let the smoke fill your space. Make sure to focus your intention on clearing any negative or stagnant energy, as well as inviting positivity and protection into your home.

Light the white candle and place it on a stable surface.

Take the clear quartz crystal and hold it in your hand. Focus on your intention to protect and promote positivity in your home. Visualise a bright, white light surrounding your home, creating a barrier of protection from negative energy and promoting positivity and love.

Take the piece of paper and write down your intention for your home. Be specific and use positive language, for example, "*My home is filled with love, light, and positivity. We are protected from negative energy and only good things come our way.*" Fold the paper and place it under the candle.

Take a small pinch of salt and sprinkle it around the candle, creating a small circle. Imagine this salt circle as a barrier of protection around the candle and your home.

Hold your crystal in your hand and speak your intention out loud. You can say something like, "*By the power of the universe, I charge this crystal to protect and promote positivity in my home. May this home be filled with love, light, and happiness. So mote it be.*"

Place the crystal in the jar or container with a lid, and seal it shut. This jar will serve as a protective talisman for your home. You can add other herbs and crystals as you wish.

Let the candle burn down completely. As it burns, continue to focus your intention on protecting and promoting positivity in your home.

Once the candle has burned out, take the jar and place it in a central location in your home. You can keep it on a shelf, in a drawer, or even bury it in your garden if you wish.

Remember to keep your intention positive and clear, and to repeat this spell as often as you feel necessary to maintain the protective and positive energy in your home.

Close your circle, thank your guides and wash your hands.

Protect Me Power Ribbon

Any

Any

Materials

A length of ribbon in a colour that represents your intention (e.g. green for healing, white for purity, orange for luck)

Scissors

A candle in a corresponding colour

A piece of paper and a pen

Instructions

Set up your sacred space, cast your circle and call on your supporters. I would go for Hecate or Kali as the most bad ass protectors, or Freya or Father Sky to tone it down a notch.

Light the candle and sit in front of it. Take a few deep breaths and focus your attention on the flame.

Take the piece of paper and write down your intention. For example: *"I attract positive energy, healing, and protection into my life."*

Cut the ribbon to a length that feels right to you. Hold the ribbon in your hands and visualise your intention as strongly as you can. See yourself surrounded by positive energy, feeling healthy and safe.

Tie a knot in the ribbon, holding your intention in mind. Repeat the intention out loud as you tie the knot.

Continue tying knots in the ribbon, repeating your intention each time, until the entire length of ribbon is filled with knots.

When you have finished, hold the ribbon (carefully) up to the candle flame and allow it to pass through the flame. As you do this, visualise the flame purifying and charging the ribbon with the power of your intention.

Hold the ribbon in your hands again and say, "*With this ribbon, I attract positivity, healing, and protection into my life. So mote it be.*"

Keep the ribbon with you or place it in a location where you will see it often, such as on your altar or tied to a piece of furniture.

Close your circle, thank your guides and wash your hands.

Whenever you see the ribbon, take a moment to repeat your intention and feel the positive energy and healing it brings. This is also a lovely gift to give to others or to attach to your little ones school bag. Feel free to use multiple coloured ribbons, create a friendship bracelet or use different materials.

Self-Love, Receiving and Detachment

We now know that manifesting your desires is a combination of creating a high vibration of abundance, positivity, and confidence. So where does self-love come into it? In order to manifest effectively, it's important to cultivate a strong connection with your inner self and develop a positive relationship with the most important person in your life- YOU!

This is where self-love is paramount and step eight in my unique process. Firstly, when you love yourself, like truly, love and respect yourself, you are more likely to believe in your own worthiness, and actually feel like you deserve to have all the things on your wish list. If deep down we don't feel like we deserve it, then guess what? We will block it. If we want to be open to receiving all the juicy stuff, we need to know that we deserve it. It doesn't mean it is taking it away from someone else, but that we are just joining the same club as those who already have it.

Secondly, having this level of relationship and connection with yourself increases your confidence and belief in your own capabilities to create the life you want. If we think that only certain people are 'good enough' or 'able enough' to manifest and be one of the 'lucky ones', we are putting a gap between 'us' and 'them'. Remember the universal law of divine oneness? We are all connected. There is no segregation in the eyes of the divine. If someone else has something the same or similar to what you desire, such as being happily married, a millionaire, successful CEO etc, then you are able to have it too. They didn't just get lucky, they got manifesting.

Self-love is also the foundation of positive energy and self-worth that attracts more positive experiences and juicy goodies into our lives. When we have a deep love for ourselves, we are able to project this love out into the world and attract loving and supportive relationships, opportunities and experiences. Remember we are a mirror and project our subconscious beliefs out into the situations and people around us, whether you like the image you are projecting or not, you do have the power to change it.

Many people struggle with self-love, and it is one of the biggest sabotaging blocks I see amongst my clients. Due to past experiences, negative self-talk and low self-esteem we can often be blinded and feel like an imposter trying to weasel in on a life that isn't meant for us. Improving your relationship with yourself, healing your soul energies and believing in your heart that you are permitted to receive requires a shift in mindset and a conscious effort to cultivate self-love. This is exactly why it is the foundation to all of the work I do, along with the other steps to manifesting we have covered in this book. Self-love is an integral piece of the puzzle. It is the core of your subconscious mind and the gateway to your 5D quantum manifesting! It can be a lifelong journey that only gets better and better as you energetically align with the person you are destined to become.

It is not about arrogance. *'She loves herself'* and *'he is so full of himself'* have been thrown around as insults for decades. But actually, this is exactly what we are aiming for. Yes, I want you to love yourself. Yes, I want your cup to be so full of you that it overflows and allows you to share yourself with others without losing yourself or burning out. There is nothing bad about this, but we are conditioned to believe it is elitist or makes us feel above other mere mortals. Please believe that this isn't the case, and you are safe to be in love with you. It is also essential, and I mean ESSENTIAL if you want to keep hold of your manifestations once they arrive. Ever got an influx of money but then received an unexpected bill a few days later? Your energetics weren't aligned but neither were your self-love, identity and self-worth. You see how everything all connects to one another?

Self-love is really about embracing all parts of yourself, including your flaws and weaknesses, and accepting yourself for who you are and where you are in your life right now. Even if you don't even like yourself on some days, or you really dislike your life at this present time, accepting it as your starting point will help you speed up your results rather than dwelling, feeling guilty or ashamed. When you love yourself, you are also less likely to be held back by self-doubt and criticisms, and more likely to attract joy and positivity into your life.

Here are some of my favourite ways to improve your relationship with yourself and become more open to receiving your desires, rather than putting up a subconscious wall in the way.

- Practice self-care: Taking care of yourself is a form of self-love. I like to think of it as the actions that lead to that ideal relationship with ourselves. Make time each day to engage in activities that bring you joy, make you feel good and that are taking care of your physical, emotional, and mental well-being. Whether it's a relaxing bath; a yoga class; a walk-in nature; attending a development workshop; a session with your coach; spending time with friends; or a good book. Make self-care a priority. It is not selfish, it is essential.

- Let go of negative self-talk: That inner critic can hold you back from manifesting your desires big style. Practice mindfulness and become aware of when you are engaging in that inner mean girl chit chat. Replace these negative thoughts with positive affirmations and focus on your strengths and achievements. Get those post it notes on your mirror, high five yourself each morning in your reflection, and tell yourself repeatedly *"I am enough. I am open to receive. I am deserving of my desires."* Record it as a voice-note and play it to yourself on your commute. Whatever works for you and allows you to reframe that conditioning.

- Surround yourself with positive people: This can sometimes be tricky to navigate but we know that the people you surround yourself with can have a big impact on your self-esteem and your ability to manifest. You may be around people who settle for a run of the mill life (in your eyes) and live each day waiting for the weekend to arrive, or who laugh at your dreams and tell you to get a grip and be realistic. These are not your people to boost your manifesting. It may not be necessary to cut them out (unless you want to, of course), but limit your contact if you can or be sure to protect yourself beforehand and give yourself a good cleanse with Palo Santo afterwards. Where possible, surround yourself with people who support and encourage you, who ask about your dreams and ambitions, and who are cheering you on from the side-lines. If you can, limit your time with those who bring you down or drain your energy like a non-sexy vampire.

- Learn to receive: Manifesting requires not only the ability to create, but also the ability to receive – both of which are a feminine energy. As **step nine** in my process, I encourage you to practice being open to receiving, whether it's in the form of compliments, gifts, or opportunities. Allow someone to open the door for you, make you a cuppa in work or let you out at a junction or crossing. The more you allow things to happen for you, the more the universe will send. How did you respond to the last compliment you received? Did you receive it with thanks, or did you deflect it with an excuse, explanation or disagreement? Play with the universe to help you get used to receiving and to practice being open. Perhaps ask to receive a free coffee, or get the parking space right next to the door. Fun things that don't have any real implications but show you that the universe will deliver if you open the door to her.

- Forgiveness: Forgive yourself and others for past mistakes and let go of grudges. Holding onto anger and resentment only blocks the flow of positive energy and abundance. If you are a woman, you will store this in your womb space and sacral centre, which will stifle your passions and creativity over time. Enjoy forgiveness rituals at the Full Moon for extra potency, but this is something you can do anytime, either through meditation, EFT, journaling, or a letter. There is also the super cool Hawaiin practice of Hoʻoponopono, which is where you say, *"I forgive you, I'm sorry, I love you."* This is one of my favourite clearing mantras for forgiveness.

- Detach from the outcome: Let go of attachment to the specific outcome of your manifestation and trust that the universe has a greater plan for you. The more you are able to trust and surrender control, the more abundance and positivity you will attract. Remember, if not this, something better is on the way. The universe will figure the logistics and the best option. If something pops up and it isn't quite right, the universe has a returns policy. Refine your intentions, submit your new order and detach as you wait for delivery. This doesn't mean you take no actions; you still do your part to move towards your goals, but you aren't dwelling on how long it is taking or doubting its arrival. **The universe always delivers.**

We know that manifesting is not about controlling the outcome, but rather about aligning yourself with your desires and trusting the universe to bring them to you. By focusing on self-love and being open to receiving, you create a higher vibration that attracts your desires to you with ease and grace. This is a journey and not a destination, nor a race, so be patient, persistent and continue to cultivate self-love every day. For extra support with this, jump in to my free Facebook group for a scrummy vibe of love and acceptance! (Search for the Resting Witch Space by Vix Marie).

Write down some daily self love ideas (or a pleasure menu) to help get you started. Be sure that these are things you can do with minimal resources so that you are not relying on having a significant amount of time or money in order to be able to enjoy them. One of my go-to activities is to cuddle one of my cats or have a hot chocolate with extra marshmallows!

My Pleasure Menu of Self Love

Aligned Action

Aligned action is a powerful aspect of your manifesting journey, and the final step in my process. This means taking inspired action (however small) that is in alignment with your intentions and goals, so you are taking steps closer to where you want to be each day. This is where you can really collapse time and reach the highest version of you in record speed.

When we set our intentions and create a vision for what we want to manifest, it is important to do our part and show the universe we mean business. This means consistency and supportive actions and behaviours, rather than being in self-destruct or sabotage mode that takes us away from where we want to be. Having a daily cheese board may sound divine but if your intention is to reduce your cholesterol and improve your heart health, this is sabotaging your goals. Enjoying a daily walk or playing in the park with your sproglets is probably more aligned. This is what we call intentional action: things that we do with purpose because we want to and know that they will support our endeavours. These are the non-negotiables that we have decided for ourselves and that our highest version of us would do without question.

We also want to allow our actions and behaviours to be inspired by our intuition and inner wisdom. This is the witch way. We don't necessarily do all of the things we 'should' because we aren't about creating overwhelm or expectations that don't feel good. Especially if you are a woman and have a fluctuating 28-day cycle that we spoke about earlier. By focusing on inspired action, we are naturally more mindful of the actions we take, as well as being open to guidance from the universe that leads us towards our goals. Take some time to listen to your inner voice and pay attention to the signs and synchronicities that show up in your life. These can be messages from the universe and your celestial team that guide you towards the right actions to take. Looking for a new job but were unsuccessful in the interview you thought was 'the one'? Look for the signs that the universe has another plan. Perhaps you see a job advertisement appear in your email inbox or receive a phone call from a recruiter, or as has happened to me, an old work colleague who just knew you were the right person for the job sends you a message.

It is important to be open to new opportunities and possibilities. When you take aligned action, you may find that many new opportunities and possibilities present themselves to you. So give yourself permission to be open to these and take advantage of them when they arise, as they may be the key to manifesting your desires. If it doesn't feel like the right opportunity, then thank the universe but ask for something more suitable. I saw this happen with my own dating experiences and also for many of my clients. I like to call them 'Test Pots' who come along and whisk us off on a date. If it isn't quite right, you are allowed to 'return to sender' and get a alternative delivered that is more suitable. It is only our fear of there being nothing else left in stock that prevents us from doing this. I promise, there will always be more stock coming.

It is also important to take consistent action towards your goals and do your bit too. This means that you need to take small steps **every** day that move you closer to your desired outcome. Consistency is key when it comes to manifesting, and taking small, consistent actions can help you build momentum. A small step every day soon adds up.

Here are some of my top tips for your action taking:

- Trust your intuition: Your intuition is your inner guidance system, and it can help you make decisions and take actions that are in alignment with your goals. A five-minute daily meditation, pulling an oracle card, or simply asking the universe and your guides what they suggest you do today can be surprisingly powerful at presenting you with ideas you may not have considered. Trust that the right actions will come to you when you are open and receptive.

- Set clear intentions: When you set clear intentions for what you want to manifest from the beginning (hence why this is step one of my process), it becomes easier to take aligned action that supports your goals. Make sure your intentions are specific and also aligned with your values and soul desires.

- Focus on the present moment: Aligned action is about taking action in the present moment that supports your goals. Focus on what you can do right now to move towards your desired outcome, rather than worrying about the future or dwelling on the past. If you have enjoyed a Moon ritual, you will notice I suggest thinking of three actions you can put into play within the next 7 days. Sometimes I will guide clients to focus on the next 24 – 48 hours instead to avoid that overwhelm of it being a long journey ahead.

- Practice self-care: I will always come back to this one and keep banging on about it (hello book two!) Taking all this action can be challenging, and it's important to take care of yourself along the way. Make sure you are getting enough sleep, eating well, and engaging in activities that bring you joy and relaxation.

- Be open to learning: Any adventure requires a willingness to learn and grow. Be open to new ideas and perspectives and be willing to make adjustments to your approach as needed. Remember growh equals fulfilment.

- Celebrate your successes: When you take action and start to see progress towards your goals, take time to celebrate your successes, no matter how big or small they are. This will help you stay motivated and keep the momentum going. Rewards charts are for grown ups too!

- Stay committed: This could be a long-term process depending on your goal, and it requires commitment and dedication. Stay focused on your goals; remind yourself *why* you want it; the importance if has in your life; that it is 100% possible for you; and keep moving, even when things get tough. Accountability buddies can help with this.

By incorporating these tips into your practice of aligned action, you can manifest your desires with more ease and success. Aligned action is about taking steps that are in supportive of your goals and desires, and it requires trust, focus, and dedication. Keep this in mind as you take action and baby steps towards your goals, and you will be well on your way to creating the life you desire.

If a fear of time management has popped up for you with all this talk of action, remember it doesn't have to be time consuming. Think about your priorities and look at how you are spending **every** minute of your day right now. Could you reallocate 5 – 10 minutes from **any** other activity to use towards a micro action that supports your goals? Accountabiliry really helps with this and as someone who used to have 3 jobs at any given time, I totally get it. Jump in to my DM's or Facebook group if you need extra help on this.

Talking of action, here is a checklist for you to complete if you wish to use my ten-step process as a guidance tool to your manifesting journey. You can also download this and some other goodies (including a womb journal) from my website at www.thewitchway.online/resources

- [ ] CLEAR INTENTION

- [ ] DECLUTTER

- [ ] ENVIRONMENT ANCHORS

- [ ] FEELINGS

- [ ] PATTERN INTERRUPT

- [ ] EXPANDERS

- [ ] TOOLS & MAGICK

- [ ] SELF LOVE

- [ ] RECEIVING

- [ ] ACTIONS

If you need a reminder and snappy summary of my process, your wish is my command:

Intention: are you sure about what it is that you want? If you are savvy with Human Design and this suggests you are a specific manifestor, this step is even more important for you. Be sure to check if your desire is genuine for you and not somebody else. It can help to think about all the reasons that you want to manifest this, as well as all the reasons that you don't. Check that it is a clear request to the universe. *This or something better.*

Decluttering: what is in the way? Either physically or mentally? Allow your emotions to guide you and signpost the changes you need. If you are wanting to release some physical weight but your wardrobe is a constant reminder of clothes you can't wear right now, it is time to clear it out. If you are looking to call in a new partner but you are still following your ex on social media, there is some mind (and potentially heart) healing to do. *What is stopping you?*

Environment: give yourself some daily prompts and reminders that your desire is coming. Use post it notes with affirmations, change your passwords, set regular alarms on your phone, update your screensaver, and incorporate incremental upgrades into your home. If I am manifesting wealth, I always have fresh flowers at home. If I am calling in new clients, I will have an alarm that pops up saying 'new sign up' - have fun with these 'anchors' that link you to your desire.

Feelings: are one of the ways your manifestations find you. How will you feel when you have received your desires? Get as specific as you can here. Once you tap into those feelings, think about other things that give you the same vibe. Incorporate those into your daily life. Does completing a puzzle give you a sense of pride like securing a promotion would do? Does watching a rom com make you feel romantic and laugh like you would in a relationship? Match up the feelings and enjoy them daily. Go deeper than surface level feelings if you can. The universe knows we all want to be happy, get specific!

Pattern Interrupts: are to be used when you feel yourself coming off track and out of alignment. This may be regular or not something you need. Come back to checking in with yourself and asking, *"Would the future me do this?"* If the answer is no - use an interrupt. You might do star-jumps, turn to your journal to write out what is going through your mind, use EFT, contact an accountability buddy, or turn to a group community to move away from the sabotage.

Expanders: who has what you want? Surround yourself with people who are in the world you are heading to. Look at their journey. How did they get there? What is their energy like? Can you replicate this? Reach out to them to speak with them or spend time with them if you can. If this isn't possible, can you follow them on social media and be immersed in their world that way? This is why coaches are great expanders too - we show you what is possible and help you get there too!

Tools and Magick: What would give your manifesting a boost? Perhaps a vision board? A placebo? The 2 cups method? Sleep manifesting? Meditation/ hypnosis? Spells?

Moon rituals? There are hundreds of different tools and magick techniques you can enjoy to bring your manifestations through faster. This is one of my favourite things to do with clients! Be sure to tailor them depending on your desire too. Scripting may work for one thing but be more challenging for another.

Self-Love: do you believe you are worthy and deserving of your desires? If we don't identify as someone who is capable of having what we want, we will either find it challenging to obtain it, or have a struggle keeping hold of it. This comes down to self-love. How can you show yourself how important, loved and deserving you are each day? The universe knows you are worthy, make sure you do too!

Receiving: are you in receiving mode? A good way to check is whenever someone compliments you or offers to help, do you take it or brush it off? Allow yourself to receive every single day. Accept someone making you a cuppa. Let someone hold the door for you or give way to you at a junction. Open that email offer and claim the voucher. Seek out the opportunities for you to receive and things will start to flow nicely.

Actions: are you behaving in alignment with your desire? If you want a relationship but you refuse to date, you are showing the universe you don't really want it. Actions can be big or small but ideally happen daily. What can you do each day to move you one step closer to your desire? Once you move, the universe will always back you. Show her you mean business! If you are unsure, ask yourself before any action, *"Would my future self do this?"*

You can follow this process in any order that you wish. I would recommend you always start with your intention but sometimes you may need to declutter your mind a little first in order to get the clarity of your desires. Some stages will be super quick for you, others a little longer or ongoing.

There is no rush; enjoy the process and the progression. Celebrate every win and every step of your journey. The fact you have made the decision to do this work consciously, with magick and grace, is utterly epic!

My Daily Practices

Meditate: whether guided, as part of a circle, when working with my vision board or just a few minutes of breathwork on the loo. This is a non negotiable to clear my mind and be present.

Affirmations: or declarations. Spoken to increase my vibe and work my throat chakra.

Nature: I always connect to the elements each day, whether it be through getting out for a walk, going swimming or setting up the firepit. This is my witchy joy!

Intentional action: what do I want to get out of today? What do I get to do? What must I do? What could I do? I will do this as a journal practice if I have time or a mental check in whilst brushing my teeth.

Feelings: how do I feel and what is this telling me? Do I need to declutter anything? What do I want to change or enhance?

Energy: do I fancy some energetic healing today? Who am I identifying as? Do I need a boost through physical activity? Do I need to rest? Is anything else influencing my energy today?

Self Love: a selected activity from my pleasure menu or self care practice for the day. Even just saying NO when I want to counts for this one.

Thanks: daily gratitude of what I am thankful for today.

What are your ideas for daily practices?

Work With Vix Marie

Warrior Coaching and Mentoring was born at the start of the global pandemic to calm the worries and concerns of women around the world. To support them in using the uncertainty and upheaval as a catalyst for change and to create the life they had only ever dreamed of before.

Providing magick mentoring and confidence coaching for wild women, closet witches, business queens and maiden goddesses, this little idea that was birthed in a paddling pool (yep, really) over a glass of prosecco in early 2020, has now become a phenomenal space of powerful transformations and manifestation.

Fully embracing her magick, owning her identity and crafting this book and accompanying oracle deck, The Witch Way was introduced as the new era of the business and a cultivation of the journey Vix Marie had endured herself on the way to owning her purpose and divine gifts. Her name now shining bright as she became her own brand!

If you have enjoyed learning about The Witch Way and want to explore this magickal world on an adventure with Vix Marie then you can join her Tribe in several ways.

For those just dipping their toe, you have the free Facebook community (and of course stalking on Instagram and TikTok too!) – jump in at www.facebook.com/groups/vixmarie and enjoy training sessions, resources and opportunities to connect with Vix Marie and your likeminded soul sisters. There are also additional downloads on her website www.thewitchway.online and you may also like to subscribe to her newsletter for the latest updates.

If you are on a healing journey and value the in person connections, you will find Vix Marie at inspring and empowering events and festivals such as Burning Woman (2023) and of course at her own in person retreats. Day sessions for womb healing, Goddess initiations, weekend sleepovers and week-long residentials take place each year across the UK (and maybe abroad soon too!)

Feeling the desire to fully immerse yourself in to the world of manifestation and dive in to your 5D quantum field? The Witch Way group coaching is a unique offering to lead you alongside other like minded women, on your evolution to the confident Goddess you are meant to be. With holistic coaching, wellbeing practices, magickal tools and mindset techniques to help you to reawaken your intuition, self belief and life potential. You will be educated and supported on this pathway of self-love as you reconnect to nature for a harmonious way of life in complete ease and flow.

For fellow coaches, entreprenuers and boss witches, you can also add on business mentoring to craft a soul led offering allowing you to shine the light for others too. With Vix Marie as your new business bestie, things will get very exciting and your success is inevitable! As a part time University Lecturer in Business Management and Marketing, you get to learn the strategy alongside the magick and woo. The perfect blend for business bliss – The Witch Way.

Regardless of your next steps, through connecting with Vix Marie you will begin to learn her unique methods, heal outdated patterns, and awaken your spiritual gifts and womb wisdom, as well as working with the elements and natural world to transform your reality.

This is The Witch Way.

Acknowledgements

Thank you to my gorgeous clients – My Tribe of Wonder Women! For all of your support over the years and for asking me for book recommendations about woo woo and manifesting which led me to create this very book – just for you. It has been an honour to be part of your journeys and I am so thankful that you are also part of mine.

To my beloved soul sisters and witchy friends who I have met along this journey. What was once a lonely path of being the outsider and the weirdo with her crystals, has now become a network of pure magick and belonging. Thank you for being a weirdo with me!

To my artistic queen, Jamie Gold. Jamie is the creatrix behind the book cover and illustrator of The Witch Way Oracle Deck (coming soon!) She explores art as a meditative practice using intuition and creative flow in connection with the spiritual world. She finds inspiration in the beauty and cycles of nature and the mysteries of the universe. I adore how she incorporates symbolism, archetypes, psychology, and colour magic into her work with the intent to elicit emotion and memory for movement in one's energy. She hopes that her art can inspire new perspectives, connections, and opportunities to grow.

For my word witch, Katie Oman, for helping me tackle how to become a writer and birth this baby in to the world. She is a book coach who helps women to create and publish their own books, whilst also being an author herself. Alongside this, Katie is a women's empowerment coach, psychic and motivational speaker.

To Danny, for the support with my ventures and bat shit crazy ideas and for the encouragement (pestering) to get this book written. For always accepting me for me- sage, incense and broomsticks included.

And of course, to you, dear reader. Thank you for being a part of my first book journey. I love you.

Love & Magick

Vix Marie
xo

Printed in Great Britain
by Amazon